COSTA RICA

A Traveler's Guide to Must-See Spots, Hidden Gems, and Insider Tips

Aria Flynn

Copyright © 2024 by Aria Flynn.
All rights reserved.
No part of this book may be reproduced, distributed, or transmitted in any form or by any means, including photocopying, recording, or other electronic or mechanical methods, without the prior written permission of the publisher, except in the case of brief quotations embodied in critical reviews and certain other noncommercial uses permitted by copyright law.

This book is a work of nonfiction. While the author has made every effort to ensure the accuracy and completeness of the information contained herein, the reader is advised that the publisher, author, and contributors are not responsible for any errors or omissions or for any consequences arising from the use of the information provided. The information contained in this book is for general guidance and educational purposes only.

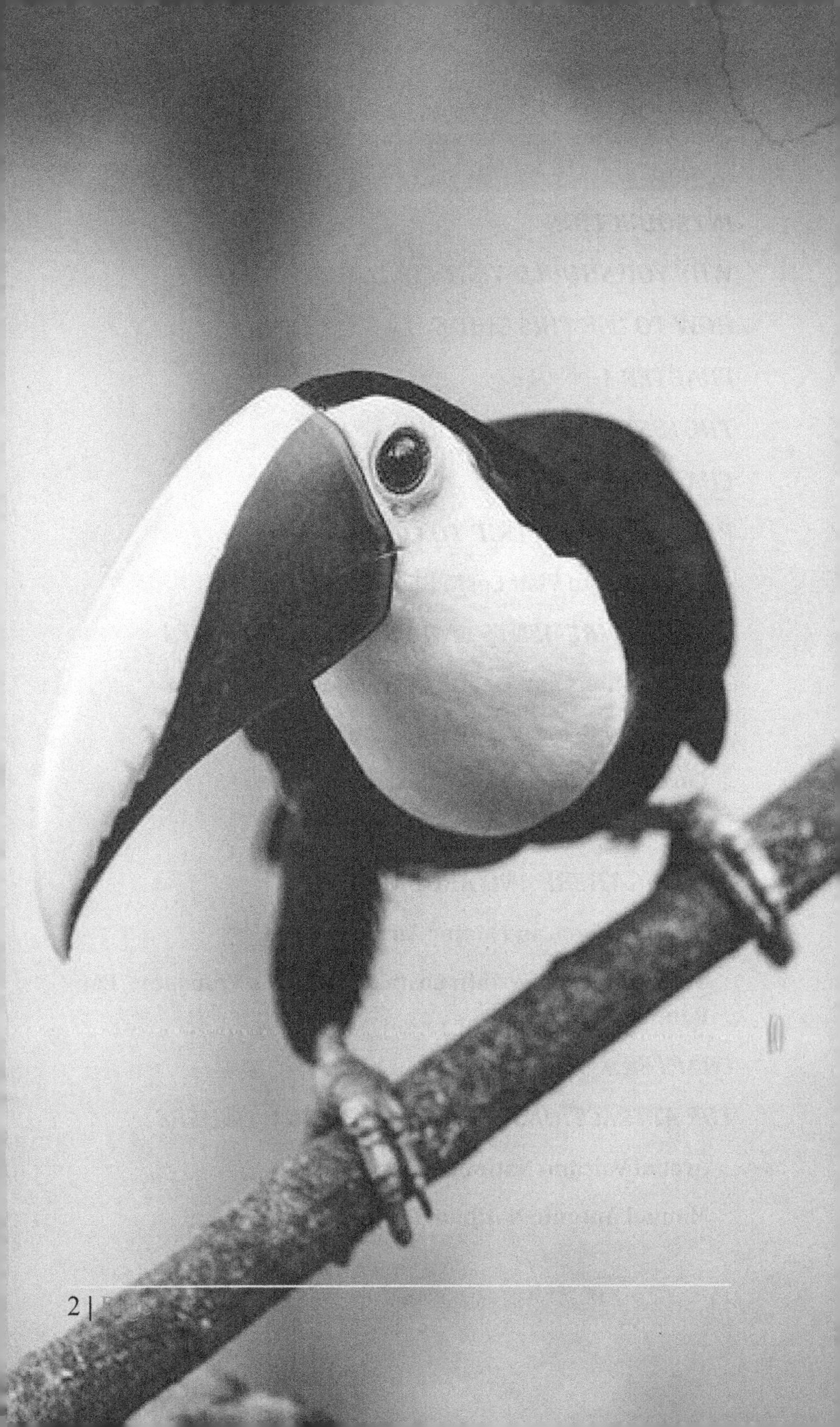

TABLE OF CONTENTS

INTRODUCTION

WHY YOU SHOULD VISIT COSTA RICA

HOW TO USE THIS GUIDE

CHAPTER 1

THE HISTORY OF COSTA RICA

CHAPTER 2

PLANNING YOUR TRIP TO COSTA RICA

   Best Time to Visit Costa Rica

VISA REQUIREMENTS AND TRAVEL DOCUMENTS

   Vaccinations and Health Precautions

   Things to Bring: Packing Essentials

   Currency, Language, and Local Etiquette

CHAPTER 3

GETTING THERE AND AROUND

   Flight Options and Major Airports

   Transportation Within Costa Rica: Public Transport, Car Rentals, and More

CHAPTER 4

TOP ATTRACTIONS AND SIGHTSEEING WONDERS

   Arenal Volcano National Park

   Manuel Antonio National Park

Monteverde Cloud Forest

Tortuguero National Park

San José

CHAPTER 5

HIDDEN GEMS

Cahuita

Rio Celeste

Santa Teresa

Barra Honda

CHAPTER 6

ADVENTURES AND ACTIVITIES

Thrilling Activities for Solo Travelers

Romantic Escapes for Couples

Family Fun

Kid-Friendly Attractions

CHAPTER 7

ACCOMMODATION OPTIONS

Luxury Resorts and Boutique Hotels

Budget-Friendly Hostels and Guesthouses

Eco-Lodges and Sustainable Stays

Family-Friendly Accommodations

Unique Stays

CHAPTER 8

GASTRONOMY AND LOCAL CUISINE

    Must-Try Costa Rican Dishes

    Best Restaurants in San José

    Food Markets and Street Eats

    Cooking Classes and Culinary Tours

CHAPTER 9

CULTURAL AND HISTORICAL INSIGHTS

    Indigenous Cultures and Traditions

    Museums, Art Galleries, and Cultural Centers

    Festivals and Events: Celebrating Costa Rican Heritage

    Architectural Landmarks and Historical Sites

CHAPTER 10

SHOPPING AND SOUVENIRS

    Markets and Artisan Crafts

    Best Places to Buy Coffee and Chocolate

CHAPTER 12

ITINERARIES FOR EVERY TRAVELER

    7-Day Itinerary for First-Time Visitors

    10-Day Itinerary for Adventure Seekers

    14-Day Itinerary for Families

CONCLUSION

MAP OF COSTA RICA

INTRODUCTION

The nation of Costa Rica, often referred to as the gem of Central America, enthralls visitors with its unique experiences, lively culture, and stunning natural surroundings. This travel book is intended to be your reliable companion, providing you with a thorough and comprehensive grasp of what makes Costa Rica such an exceptional place, whether you are organizing your first trip or returning for another adventure.

You'll quickly learn that Costa Rica is much more than simply a tropical paradise when you make travel plans. From verdant rainforests and foggy cloud forests to active volcanoes, breathtaking beaches, and vast marshes, the nation's landscapes are very varied. This guide will assist you in exploring each location according to your interests and preferred method of travel. Every region of Costa Rica has something unique to offer, from the serene Caribbean shoreline to the untamed beauty of the Pacific coast.

Costa Rica's dedication to environmental preservation is among the first things one learns about the country. With almost 25% of its territory preserved in national parks and reserves, the nation is well known for its conservation efforts. Wildlife such as howler monkeys, sloths, toucans, and the recognizable blue morpho butterfly have found refuge in Costa Rica as a result of this commitment to the environment. Given the abundance of possibilities to see these animals in their native environments, nature lovers will enjoy this place.

You will be in awe of the nation's natural treasures whether you decide to trek through a rainforest, go on a guided animal trip, or just unwind in a hot spring.

The allure of Costa Rica extends beyond its natural beauty and fauna. A combination of Spanish colonial influences, indigenous roots, and contemporary advancements have molded the nation's history and culture, which are equally intriguing. This rich cultural fabric is evident in the architecture, celebrations, and daily lives of the locals as you go through cities and villages.

With its museums, theaters, and historical sites that provide a window into the nation's history and present, San José, the capital, is a center of cultural activity. You may visit the majestic National Theater, a representation of Costa Rica's creative legacy, or tour the National Museum, which has pre-Columbian items.

Costa Rica has a wide range of adventure-oriented activities that appeal to both thrill-seekers and those seeking more relaxed pastimes. Because of its diverse landscape, the nation is perfect for sports like scuba diving, surfing, white-water rafting, and zip-lining. There are also many of chances for horseback riding, bird viewing, or just lounging on one of the numerous immaculate beaches if you'd rather do something more laid-back. This book will provide you comprehensive information on how to make the most of your stay in Costa Rica, regardless of your interests, so that your vacation is rewarding and unforgettable.

In Costa Rica, lodging alternatives are as varied as the country's surroundings. This guide will assist you in finding the ideal lodging option, whether you're searching for family-friendly hotels, affordable hostels, comfortable eco-lodges, or opulent resorts. Whether you're staying in a quaint mountain refuge, waking up to the sounds of the rainforest, or enjoying views of the ocean from your room, every kind of lodging provides a different experience. The book also offers helpful advice on things to consider when selecting a place to stay, including location, accessibility, and facilities and services.

In terms of gastronomy, Costa Rica's rich natural resources and cultural variety are reflected in it. Simple but tasty, the nation's cuisine often uses fresh ingredients including rice, beans, plantains, and tropical fruits. This book will introduce you to some of the must-try foods, such ceviche (fresh fish marinated in lime juice), casado (a classic lunch plate), and gallo pinto (a traditional breakfast meal of rice and beans). The greatest places to dine will also be covered, ranging from more expensive eating institutions to neighborhood sodas, which are tiny, family-run eateries.

This book offers comprehensive details on lodgings, activities, and sites in addition to important travel advice to make sure you have a smooth trip across Costa Rica. Advice on anything from safety guidelines and transit alternatives to health precautions and visa requirements may be found here. This book will make sure you have all the information you need for a hassle-free and joyful journey, regardless of whether you're traveling alone, with a spouse, children, or a family.

You will learn more about what makes Costa Rica so unique as you read through the pages of this book. Whether you're here for a quick trip or a longer stay, the country's stunning natural surroundings, vibrant culture, and friendly people will make an effect on you that will remain. This book is an essential tool for anybody planning a vacation to Costa Rica since it is full with insightful information and useful suggestions.

Therefore, this book will be your key to unlocking the numerous secrets that Costa Rica has to offer, whether your dreams include exploring lush rainforests, lounging on sun-kissed beaches, or fully immersing yourself in the lively culture. Prepare yourself for an amazing trip to one of the world's most beautiful and hospitable nations. Costa Rica awaits your exploration, and this guide will help you enjoy every second of your journey.

WHY YOU SHOULD VISIT COSTA RICA

Visitors from all over the globe have fallen in love with Costa Rica, and with good cause. The amazing combination of Costa Rica's rich culture, stunning natural surroundings, and friendly people are the main reasons to go there. For everyone wishing to see the beauties of our world, this little but diversified country is a must-visit since it provides a unique experience that is difficult to obtain anywhere.

First and foremost, the natural scenery of Costa Rica is just amazing. Despite its tiny size, the nation is home to some of the planet's most varied ecosystems. Costa Rica provides a broad range of habitats that appeal to all types of tourists, from the clean beaches that run down the Pacific and Caribbean shores to the deep jungles filled with animals. Costa Rica has something for everyone, whether you're an adventurer hoping to walk up a volcano, a nature lover hoping to see exotic creatures in the wild, or someone who just wants to unwind by the sea.

Costa Rica's commitment to protecting the environment is among its most impressive features. With almost 25% of its territory set aside as national parks, reserves, and wildlife refuges, the nation has achieved great strides in safeguarding its natural resources. Because of this dedication to conservation, tourists may enjoy the splendor of unspoiled environment in a manner that is becoming more and more uncommon in our contemporary society. From the vibrant birds that fly through the trees to the monkeys who swing from branch to limb, these protected areas provide an astounding display of variety. Observing these animals in their native environment is an unforgettable experience that enhances your respect for the natural world.

Among the greatest adventure sports in the world, Costa Rica is also well-known for them. The alternatives accessible here will not let you down if you want a good thrill. Whether zip-lining through a rainforest canopy, rafting down a raging river, or exploring enigmatic caverns, the nation's diverse geography provides many chances for adventure. You may go from surfing on a tropical beach one day to trekking through a cloud forest the next because the terrain is so varied. In addition to offering thrill, these activities provide you a unique and immersive opportunity to take in Costa Rica's natural beauty.

However, Costa Rica is a nation rich in culture and history, so it's not only about adventure and the outdoors. Ticos, or Costa Ricans, are proud of their culture and want to share it with tourists. You will get the chance to discover more about the indigenous civilizations that have inhabited this nation for generations as you go throughout it. You may tour museums that highlight the history and art of the area, take part in traditional festivals, and visit historic archeological sites. This cultural diversity enhances your trip and helps you establish a stronger bond with the nation.

Costa Rica is a place that provides a good standard of living in addition to its natural and cultural attractions. The nation is renowned for its peaceful culture, stable democracy, and focus on healthcare and education. In Costa Rica, the expression "Pura Vida," which means "pure life," is more than simply a catchphrase; it's a way of life. Visitors soon notice and enjoy this upbeat and laid-back atmosphere. Known for their warmth and friendliness, the Ticos will make you feel at home as soon as you get there. Costa Ricans are always willing to offer their warmth and compassion, whether you're dining at a family-run restaurant or striking up a conversation with neighbors in a tiny town.

Another incentive to go to Costa Rica is its cuisine. Simple, fresh, and tasty food is served here, often made using ingredients that are farmed and collected nearby. Traditional foods like gallo pinto, a tasty combination of rice and beans that is often eaten with plantains and eggs for breakfast, will be available for you to sample. There are many possibilities to try ceviche, a meal created from marinated raw fish, and fresh seafood is plentiful, particularly in coastal locations. You may enjoy fresh juices and smoothies prepared from mangoes, pineapples, and other tropical fruits since they are so abundant. In Costa Rica, eating is more than simply a way to satisfy your hunger; it's also a way to experience the local cuisine and culture.

Costa Rica is a great place for families to go. With a variety of family-friendly activities that suit all ages, the nation is renowned for being safe. There are many methods to keep kids interested and delighted, whether it's a visit to a butterfly garden, a boat trip to view dolphins, or a day spent at a wildlife rescue facility. Additionally noteworthy are the educational possibilities; children may study biology, ecology, and conservation in a practical setting that brings these topics to life. Family travel to Costa Rica is a fulfilling experience that leaves parents and kids with priceless memories.

Additionally, Costa Rica is a fantastic place for singles and couples to visit. The nation is ideal for couples wishing to go away and re-connect because of its romantic locations, which include remote beaches and verdant jungles. There are many romantic possibilities in Costa Rica, whether you're planning a honeymoon, anniversary trip, or simply a romantic vacation. With a robust infrastructure that makes getting about easy, the nation is friendly and accessible to lone travelers. Costa Rica is a great option for solo travelers because of the feeling of adventure, the possibility to interact with other tourists, and the chance to fully experience the native way of life.

Another allure of the nation is its environment, which has pleasant temperatures all year round and a range of microclimates depending on where you travel. There is a climate to fit your tastes, whether you want the damp richness of the jungle or the dry heat of the Pacific coast. Regardless of the time of year you choose to go, there is always a good time to visit Costa Rica because of its diverse temperature.

Lastly, Costa Rica is a location where you may really detach yourself from the strains of daily life and rediscover what's important. A feeling of rest and rejuvenation is facilitated by the tranquil surroundings, the slower pace of life, and the beauty of nature. Costa Rica has the ability to make you feel comfortable and at home, whether you're sitting in a café taking in the scenery, trekking through a jungle, or just relaxing on a beach.

From breathtaking natural scenery and exhilarating activities to rich cultural experiences and friendly locals, Costa Rica has something to offer everyone. All of these factors work together to create it a destination that you will want to visit and return to throughout your life. Costa Rica is a place that provides whether you're seeking for adventure, leisure, education, or a combination of all three. It is a place where the kindness of the people, the diversity of culture, and the beauty of the natural world all combine to make for a really remarkable vacation.

HOW TO USE THIS GUIDE

This guide is designed to be your comprehensive companion as you plan and experience your first trip to Costa Rica. Whether you're seeking adventure, relaxation, or cultural exploration, this book provides all the essential information you need to make your journey unforgettable. Here's how to make the most of this guide:

Getting Started with Planning
Begin by familiarizing yourself with the introductory chapters. These sections offer valuable insights into the best times to visit, the country's climate, and essential travel documents like visas and vaccinations. Understanding these basics will help you plan your trip with confidence, ensuring that you arrive prepared and ready to explore.

Exploring Top Attractions and Hidden Gems
The core of this guide is dedicated to exploring Costa Rica's most popular destinations, as well as the lesser-known gems that make the country so special. Each destination is described in detail, with highlights on what to see, do, and experience. Use this section to create your itinerary, selecting the places that resonate most with your interests and travel style. Whether you're drawn to the vibrant wildlife of Tortuguero, the volcanic landscapes of Arenal, or the pristine beaches of Manuel Antonio, this guide provides all the information you need to plan your days.

Tailoring Your Experience

To help you make the most of your trip, this guide includes tailored itineraries for different types of travelers. Whether you're a solo adventurer, a couple seeking a romantic getaway, or a family with children, these itineraries offer curated suggestions that suit your specific needs. Feel free to mix and match activities and destinations from different itineraries to create a personalized travel plan.

Essential Travel Tips

Throughout the guide, you'll find practical advice on everything from packing essentials to transportation options within Costa Rica. These tips are designed to help you navigate the country smoothly, avoid common pitfalls, and ensure your safety and comfort. Pay close attention to these sections to enhance your overall travel experience.

Cultural Insights and Local Etiquette

Costa Rica is a country with a rich cultural heritage and friendly locals who take pride in their traditions. To help you connect with the culture and show respect to the people you'll meet, this guide includes sections on language, local customs, and etiquette. Understanding these cultural nuances will enrich your interactions and make your visit more meaningful.

Accommodation and Dining Recommendations

Finding the right place to stay and the best spots to eat can significantly impact your travel experience. This guide offers recommendations for a wide range of accommodation options, from luxury resorts to budget-friendly hostels. It also highlights must-try local dishes and the best places to enjoy Costa Rican cuisine, ensuring that your stay is both comfortable and delicious.

Adventure Activities and Nature Experiences
Costa Rica is renowned for its outdoor adventures and natural beauty. This guide provides detailed information on the country's top activities, including zip-lining, whitewater rafting, hiking, and wildlife watching. Use this section to discover the best adventure opportunities and plan exciting excursions that align with your interests and energy levels.

Interactive Features and Maps
To help you navigate Costa Rica with ease, this guide includes a QR code. Simply scan the QR codes provided throughout the book using your smartphone or tablet, and you'll be instantly directed to the exact locations of key attractions, accommodations, restaurants, and more. These QR code is to be user-friendly, offering clear and precise directions that make exploring Costa Rica more convenient. Whether you're plotting your route to a hidden waterfall or finding the best place to enjoy a local meal, the QR code will ensure you have the information you need right at your fingertips.

Staying Flexible
While this guide offers a wealth of information and carefully crafted itineraries, it's important to stay flexible and open to new experiences. Costa Rica is a country full of surprises,

and some of the best moments happen when you least expect them. Use this guide as a roadmap, but don't be afraid to venture off the beaten path and discover something new.

By following the advice and recommendations in this guide, you'll be well-equipped to experience the very best that Costa Rica has to offer. Whether you're marveling at the biodiversity of the rainforests, soaking in natural hot springs, or connecting with the local culture, this guide is here to ensure that your first visit to Costa Rica is nothing short of extraordinary.

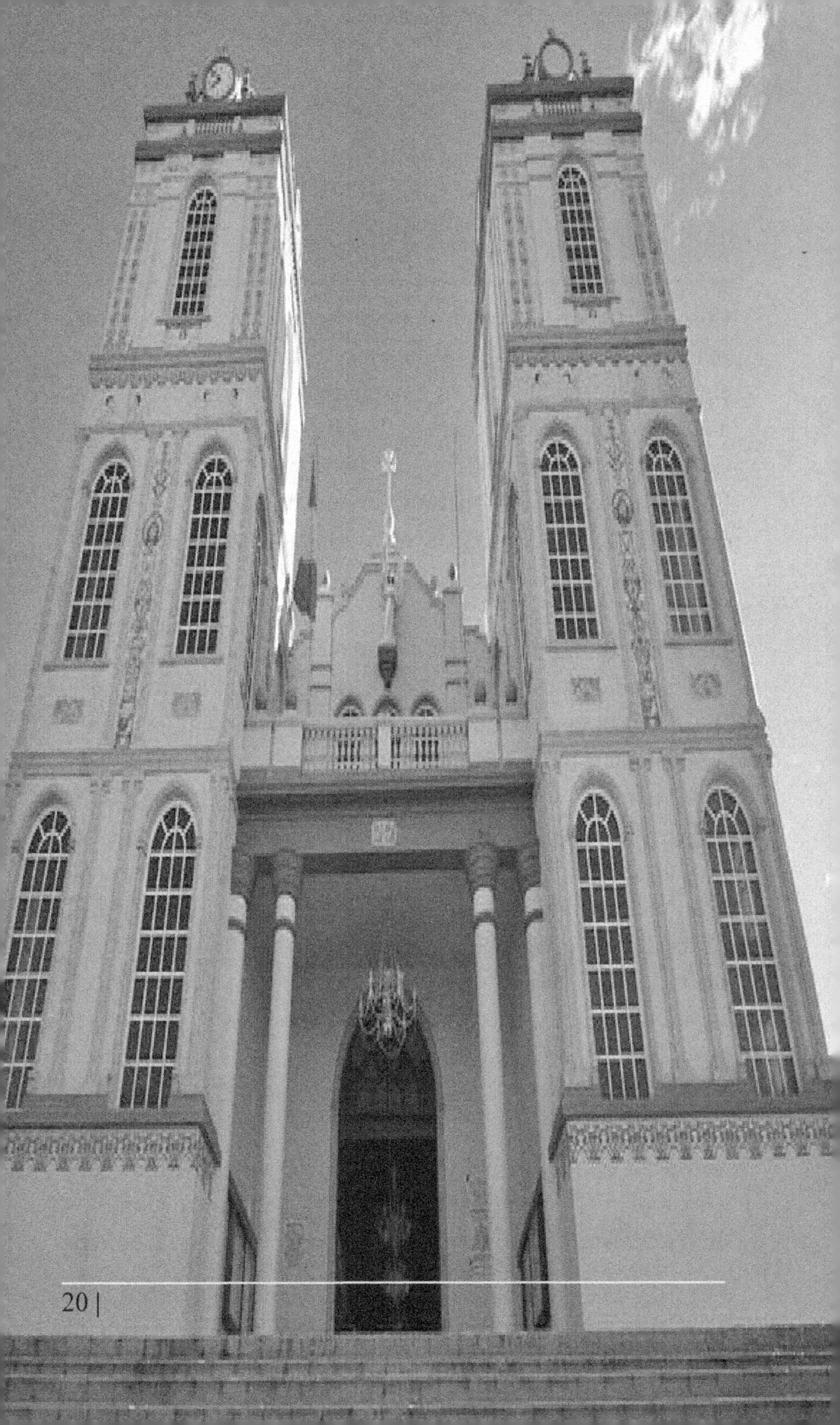

CHAPTER 1

THE HISTORY OF COSTA RICA

Costa Rica is a peaceful, democratic country with a strong sense of identity and a dedication to protecting its natural environment. Its history is a complex tapestry of events that have fashioned the country into what it is today. Knowing Costa Rica's history helps us understand how this little Central American nation came to be what it is and why it is different in an area that is often characterized by political unrest and war.

Long before European settlers arrived, Costa Rica's history began. Indigenous peoples first settled in what is now Costa Rica, and they established sophisticated communities with a wealth of customs and cultures. The greater Mesoamerican and Isthmo-Colombian cultural regions, which comprised societies renowned for their innovations in commerce, agriculture, and ceramics, included these early occupants. With their own unique languages, rituals, and social systems, Costa Rica's indigenous groups—including the Chorotega, Bribri, and Cabécar—lived in tiny settlements dispersed across the country. In addition to cultivating crops like maize, beans, and chocolate, they traded with other communities, trading commodities like gold, pottery, and jade.

European exploration of the area began in 1502 with Christopher Columbus's arrival. On his fourth expedition to the New World, Columbus set foot on Costa Rica's eastern coast, close to the present-day town of Limón. The land's natural beauty and the seeming affluence of the native inhabitants, who decked themselves out in gold trinkets, both impressed him. Because of this, Columbus gave the region the name "Costa Rica," which translates to "Rich Coast." However, the process of colonization in Costa Rica was longer and less successful than in other regions of the Americas, and the riches that Columbus and other explorers thought to discover in abundance did not exist in the amounts they had expected.

Although it was a difficult process, Spanish colonization of Costa Rica formally started in the early 16th century. The region's hard topography, which included marshes, rocky mountains, and deep woods, made it difficult for the Spanish to establish authority, and the native populations opposed the Spanish intrusions. Spain benefited greatly from the conquests of the Inca and Aztec empires, but the colonization of Costa Rica was less profitable. The Spanish crown mostly disregarded the region in favor of places like Mexico and Peru that had more immediate economic prospects.

Costa Rica became a quite remote and independent colony as a consequence. The majority of the immigrants who did arrive in Costa Rica were impoverished Spanish workers and farmers who had to depend on their own ingenuity to make ends meet. They founded tiny farming settlements, rearing cattle and cultivating crops including sugarcane, tobacco, and chocolate. A less hierarchical and more egalitarian society than in other regions of Spanish America resulted from the immigrants' gradual intermarriage with the native population. Costa Rica did not establish the massive plantations or encomiendas (land concessions) that were typical in other colonies due to a lack of important natural resources and sizable indigenous labor forces.

The Central Valley, which became the center of Costa Rican civilization, witnessed the establishment of new cities and communities throughout the colony's slow growth in the 18th century. This area became the epicenter of coffee production in the 19th century due to its rich soil and temperate temperature, which made it perfect for cultivation. In the end, coffee would emerge as Costa Rica's most significant export, propelling economic expansion and influencing national progress.

When all of Central America proclaimed their independence from Spain in 1821, Costa Rica too became free of Spanish domination. But there were difficulties along the way to Costa Rican nationhood. The United Provinces of Central America, the federation that the newly independent provinces of Central America first established, was beset by internal strife and disputes. In 1838, Costa Rica, which had always been somewhat cut off from the rest of the area, made the decision to become an independent republic and break away from the federation.

Efforts to create a stable and successful country characterized the early years of Costa Rican independence. The expansion of the coffee business was one of the major events of this time. As a source of revenue and a way to integrate the nation into the global economy, coffee emerged as the mainstay of the Costa Rican economy. A new elite class of coffee producers emerged as a result of the coffee boom, and they had a big influence on the political and social climate of the nation.

Another significant facet of Costa Rica's history is its dedication to democracy and education. Leaders in Costa Rica realized the value of education in creating a strong, united community around the middle of the 19th century. The nation made investments in public education, building colleges and institutions that were open to all residents. A stable and democratic political structure was developed as a result of the focus on education, which also helped to produce a populace that was knowledgeable and literate.

The outbreak of a short-lived but bloody civil war in 1948 in reaction to a contentious presidential election was one of the most pivotal events in Costa Rican history. A new administration headed by José Figueres Ferrer was installed after the government troops were defeated in the short 44-day conflict. Figueres, who would go on to become one of Costa Rica's most powerful presidents, took the risky choice to disband the nation's military, which has had a significant effect on Costa Rican culture. Costa Rica was able to refocus resources on social programs, healthcare, and education by dismantling the military, which strengthened its democratic institutions and fostered a culture of peace.

Since the military was abolished, Costa Rica has been seen as a symbol of democracy and stability in Central America. It has continuously been rated as one of the world's most peaceful and democratic countries, avoiding the civil wars, dictatorships, and conflicts that have beset many of its neighbors. Costa Rica has gained respect and reputation across the world for its dedication to social welfare, environmental preservation, and human rights.

Costa Rica kept growing its economy, diversifying its exports, and growing its tourist sector throughout the second half of the 20th century. Travelers from all over the globe have found the country to be a popular destination due to its natural beauty, political stability, and friendly attitude. One of Costa Rica's most vital sectors today, tourism supports thousands of employments and makes a substantial economic contribution to the nation.

The history of Costa Rica is one of tenacity, ingenuity, and a strong dedication to democracy and peace. Costa Rica has always forged its own path, driven by the ideals of equality, education, and environmental care, from its beginnings as a distant and isolated colony to its rise as a modern and wealthy country. Both Costa Ricans and tourists are still motivated by the nation's distinctive past, which has molded its national character.

Gaining knowledge about Costa Rica's past enables us to grasp its current successes and difficulties. It serves as a reminder that centuries of toil, tough choices, and a shared dedication to creating a better future have led to the peace and prosperity Costa Rica enjoys today. The remnants of this past can be seen everywhere in Costa Rica, whether in its people, culture, or scenery, giving you a greater appreciation for what makes this nation unique.

CHAPTER 2

PLANNING YOUR TRIP TO COSTA RICA

Best Time to Visit Costa Rica

Because Costa Rica's temperature fluctuates drastically throughout the year and offers varied possibilities depending on the season, the ideal time to visit depends on what you are looking for. Because of its Central American position, Costa Rica has a tropical climate, meaning that temperatures are often warm all year round. The nation does, however, have distinct rainy and dry seasons, which may have a big influence on your experiences and vacation plans.

The most popular period to visit Costa Rica is during the dry season, which lasts from December to April. You can anticipate plenty of sunlight and minimal rain throughout these months, which makes them perfect for outdoor pursuits like hiking, animal viewing, and beachcombing. For individuals who want to visit the nation's national parks, the dry season is especially alluring because of the easier access to trails and improved visibility of animals due to the absence of rain. With sunny days and chilly evenings, the Pacific coast in particular has almost perfect weather at this time of year, making it the perfect time to surf, sunbathe, and explore coastal villages.

Popular tourist locations like Manuel Antonio, Arenal, and Monteverde may see increased traffic and crowding during the dry season, which also happens to be the busiest time of year. If you want to travel during these months, it is best to make reservations in advance since accommodations and excursions tend to fill up fast. Many tourists find that the dry season is well worth the expense since it is the period when they are most likely to see unbroken sunlight, even though it is often more expensive owing to high demand.

The rainy season, also referred to as the "green season," which runs from May to November, has its own distinct attraction despite the popularity of the dry season. Mornings are often bright and clear throughout this period, but the country gets more regular rain showers, especially in the afternoons. With the trees and plants thriving in the dampness, Costa Rica's sceneries are transformed into a lush, colorful paradise during the rainy season. Visitors have the opportunity to see Costa Rica's splendor in full bloom during this season, when the nation's flora and animals really come to life.

One of the main advantages of going during the rainy season is that there are less visitors, so you may see well-known sights without having to deal with large crowds. Because lodging and excursions are less expensive at this period, it's a desirable choice for those on a tight budget. Furthermore, the rain causes the landscape to alter dramatically, with rivers swell, waterfalls becoming stronger, and the rainforest turning a deeper, more vivid shade of green. The rainy season is a unique chance for photographers and wildlife enthusiasts to document Costa Rica's landscapes in their most colorful and dynamic form.

Although there is more rain during the rainy season, it is crucial to remember that the weather varies around the nation. For instance, the weather pattern in the Caribbean coast differs from that of the rest of the nation, with more constant rainfall all year round. However, September and October are often the driest months in this region, making them ideal travel months if you want to see places like Tortuguero or Cahuita. With its Afro-Caribbean culture, immaculate beaches, and a wealth of animals, the Caribbean coast provides a distinct side of Costa Rica, but with less reliable weather.

The many festivals and events that occur all year long should also be taken into account when organizing your trip. Numerous religious and cultural festivals are held in Costa Rica, many of which have their roots in the nation's history and customs. For instance, one of the most well-liked occasions in San José is the Fiestas de Zapote, which happens in late December and includes traditional cuisine, live music, and bullfights. Another important period is Holy Week, also known as Semana Santa, when religious festivities and processions are held in numerous towns and cities. You may get a unique and immersive perspective of Costa Rican culture by traveling there during these periods.

There are transitional times, especially between May and November, when the weather is more erratic, in addition to the dry and rainy seasons. Known as the "shoulder seasons," these months might provide tourists with a little bit of both worlds by combining dry and rainy weather. If you want to escape the busiest times of year while still taking advantage of good weather, the shoulder seasons might be great times to go.

The particular activities you choose to partake in may help determine the ideal time of year to visit Costa Rica. For instance, the greatest time to go to the Pacific coast if you want to see whales is during the migratory seasons, which run from July to October and again from January to March. Visitors may see a unique and stunning sight as humpback whales migrate from the northern and southern hemispheres to the warm seas of Costa Rica during these months to give birth. Another unique time to visit is during turtle breeding season, which varies according on the species. The Caribbean coast's Tortuguero National Park is well-known for its green sea turtle breeding season, which runs from July to October.

Another activity where the season has a significant impact is surfing. Along the Pacific coast, the dry season brings steady waves, especially at well-known surfing locations like Tamarindo and Santa Teresa. However, bigger waves during the rainy season might draw more seasoned surfers seeking a challenge. The best waves are usually found from November to March on the Caribbean coast, which also has its own surf season. All year long, there are waves for surfers of all ability levels, regardless of experience level.

Although Costa Rica is a year-round destination for bird watchers, there are certain special chances during specific seasons. There is a lot of bird activity in the woodlands during the rainy season, especially from May to July, when many bird species nest. Additionally, migrating birds from North America arrive in Costa Rica around this season, increasing the variety of species that may be seen. For those who prefer more agreeable weather, the drier months of December through April are ideal since they provide better sky and easier access to bird-watching locations.

The ideal time to go to Costa Rica will depend on your interests and the experiences you want to have while there. Costa Rica is a year-round destination because of its abundance of natural beauty, adventure, and cultural experiences, regardless of whether you decide to go there during the sunny dry season or the lush green season. You may arrange a vacation that suits your interests and guarantees a fulfilling and unforgettable experience by being aware of the subtleties of the nation's climate and the range of activities offered all year long.

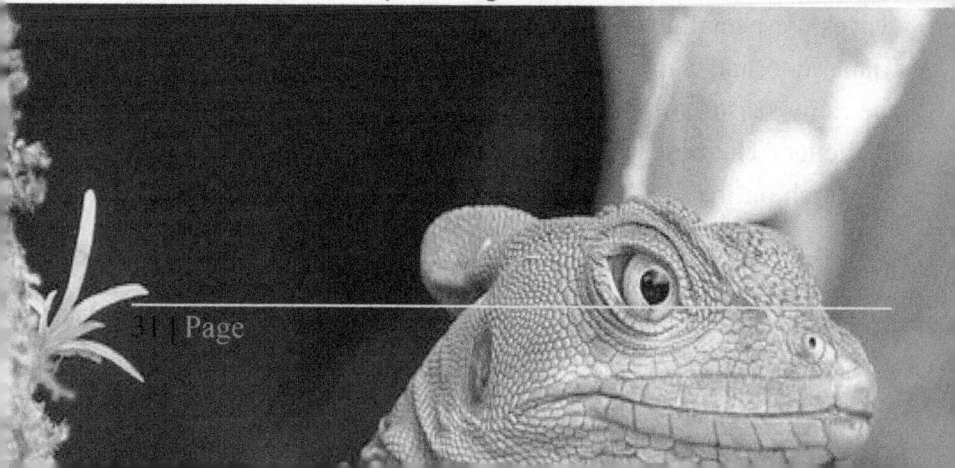

VISA REQUIREMENTS AND TRAVEL DOCUMENTS

To guarantee a seamless and trouble-free vacation to Costa Rica, it is crucial to comprehend the visa requirements and required travel papers. Costa Rica, which is renowned for its warm and inviting environment, has set down explicit rules for visitors to enter the nation. The duration of your stay, the reason for your visit, and your nationality all affect these rules. To prevent any issues at the border, it's crucial to get aware with these criteria well in advance of your journey.

For the majority of tourists, traveling to Costa Rica is rather simple. For brief visits, citizens of a number of nations, including the US, Canada, the majority of EU countries, and numerous more, do not need a visa to enter Costa Rica. You may enter Costa Rica for up to 90 days without a visa if you are a citizen of one of these nations. Even if you may not need a visa, you still need to complete certain requirements and provide certain papers in order to get entrance.

A valid passport is the most important document you will need. In addition to being in excellent shape, your passport must still be valid for at least six months after the date of your arrival in Costa Rica. You could not be allowed admission if your passport expires within six months since this restriction is carefully enforced. Checking your passport's expiry date well in advance of your intended trip and renewing it if needed is always a smart idea.

You must provide documentation of further or return travel in addition to your passport. This implies that a ticket indicating your intention to depart Costa Rica prior to the end of your 90-day tourist term is required. This might be a ticket to another country or a ticket back to your native country. This restriction is strictly enforced by Costa Rican immigration officials in order to prevent tourists from staying in the nation for longer than permitted. You can be asked to buy a return ticket right away before being permitted admission if you arrive in Costa Rica without documentation of your intended itinerary.

The reason for your visit is another crucial factor to take into account. You should travel for pleasure, vacation, or other non-work-related purposes since the 90-day visa-free entrance is only for tourists. Before visiting Costa Rica, you must get the necessary visa if you want to work in any capacity, whether for pay or not. Working without the appropriate visa may lead to penalties, deportation, and a ban from entering the nation again.

Travelers who do not originate from nations that do not need visas will need to apply for a tourist visa. You must apply at the closest Costa Rican embassy or consulate in your home country if you need a visa in order to visit Costa Rica. Your passport, a filled-out application form, passport-sized photos, evidence of having enough money to finance your stay, and proof of future travel are usually required for the visa application procedure. Other documents, such a letter of invitation or proof of lodging during your visit, can also be requested by the embassy.

Applying for a tourist visa well in advance of the day you want to go is crucial since processing times might vary. An in-person interview may sometimes be required by the embassy as a component of the application procedure. You will be able to enter Costa Rica after your visa has been accepted and stamped in your passport. Be ready to respond to inquiries regarding your trip itinerary and provide proof of your return ticket since, even with a visa, you can still be subject to further inspections when you get to Costa Rica.

Travel needs connected to health are another crucial factor to take into account. Even though admission into Costa Rica usually doesn't need vaccines, it's a good idea to check for any health warnings or immunization recommendations before you arrive. For instance, you could be asked to provide documentation of your yellow fever vaccine if you are traveling from a place where the disease is a concern. This is especially important for tourists who have recently been to South American or African nations where yellow fever is a problem. The certificate of immunization against yellow fever must be obtained at least ten days before to travel to Costa Rica.

Although it is not required, travel insurance is strongly advised before visiting Costa Rica. The healthcare system in Costa Rica is excellent, although it may be expensive, particularly for visitors. In the event of sickness or accidents while traveling, having travel insurance that covers emergency evacuation, medical costs, and other unforeseen circumstances may provide you peace of mind and shield you from heavy financial responsibilities. In the event that your plans suddenly alter, some travel insurance packages also cover lost baggage, delays, and trip cancellations.

Another crucial component of visiting Costa Rica is adhering to customs laws. You will need to complete a customs declaration form when you arrive. If you are bringing cash, gadgets, or other valuables into the nation, you will be asked to declare them on this form. Some things are restricted; for example, illicit narcotics, guns, and ammunition are all absolutely forbidden. You could have to pay customs charges if you are bringing in goods like alcohol or tobacco that are more than the duty-free allowed.

Additionally, you can be questioned about your lodging plans when you first arrive in Costa Rica. The address of the hotel or other location you will be staying at should be easily accessible. You can be asked for their contact details if you are staying with friends or relatives. Your trip itinerary, including the places you plan to visit and the length of time you plan to remain in each place, may be questioned by immigration officials. Answers that are succinct and easy to understand may speed up the admission process.

It's also important to remember that Costa Rica takes environmental preservation extremely seriously. To stop the introduction of pests and illnesses that may damage the local ecology, the nation maintains stringent laws governing the importation of food items, plants, and animals. You may have to disclose and have agricultural officials check any of these products if you are bringing them into the nation. Fines and the seizure of the forbidden goods may follow noncompliance with these rules.

Lastly, while departing Costa Rica, it's essential to understand the departure formalities. You must pay an exit tax before you may board your aircraft if you are traveling outside of the nation. This fee, which typically costs around $29, may be paid with cash or a credit card at the airport. It's a good idea to verify with your airline before booking your trip since some include this tax in the ticket price. Make sure you have enough time to pay the tax at the airport before passing through security if it is not covered by your ticket.

Travel documentation and visa requirements must be carefully considered while visiting Costa Rica as a tourist. It will be easier and less stressful to enter the nation if you have documentation of future travel, make sure your passport is valid, and are aware of the health and customs laws. Having the appropriate paperwork in place will let you to concentrate on taking in everything that Costa Rica has to offer, whether you are visiting for a quick trip or a longer stay. Your vacation to Costa Rica may be an interesting and unforgettable experience if you plan ahead and prepare properly.

Vaccinations and Health Precautions

To guarantee a safe and healthy journey, immunizations and health measures should be taken into account while making travel plans to Costa Rica. Costa Rica is renowned for its biodiversity and natural beauty, so even if there aren't many health hazards there, there are still some crucial safety measures to follow. You may enjoy your vacation without needless worries if you are aware of the nation's health situation and have the required immunizations and precautions.

There are excellent medical facilities in cities and popular tourist locations, and Costa Rica's healthcare system is well recognized and easily accessible. However, it's important to take precautions to shield yourself from any health dangers, just as with any foreign trip. Speaking with a medical expert or travel clinic a few weeks before your trip is recommended. This will provide enough time to get any necessary immunizations and learn about travel health precautions.

The hepatitis A vaccine is among the most often advised immunizations for visitors visiting Costa Rica. Hepatitis A is a liver-damaging viral illness that is often spread via tainted food or water. Even though there isn't much chance of getting hepatitis A in Costa Rica—especially if you practice proper hygiene—vaccination is advised as a precaution. The initial dosage of the vaccination offers the most protection, and it is often given in two doses spaced six months apart.

The hepatitis B vaccine is another often recommended

immunization. Another viral illness that damages the liver is hepatitis B, which is spread by coming into touch with contaminated blood or body fluids. Most visitors have a minimal chance of contracting hepatitis B, particularly if they are not participating in activities that may expose them to blood, such getting a tattoo or having medical procedures done. Nonetheless, vaccination is still advised, particularly if you intend to remain in Costa Rica for an extended period of time or if you are likely interact closely with locals. Usually, three shots spaced out over six months are used to provide the hepatitis B vaccination.

Another risk for visitors to Costa Rica is typhoid illness, especially if they intend to consume street food or go to rural regions. Bacteria cause typhoid, which is transmitted by tainted food and drink. For individuals who choose to take additional measures, immunization is advised even though the danger is normally minimal in the majority of Costa Rica. The typhoid vaccination comes in two forms: an injection that lasts up to two years or an oral vaccine that is given as a series of capsules over the course of a week.

Although there isn't a large danger of malaria in Costa Rica, it's still a good idea to talk to your doctor about malaria prevention if you want to go to any rural or forest regions, especially those that are close to the Caribbean coast or the Nicaraguan border. If left untreated, malaria, a disease spread by mosquitoes, may result in severe sickness. Preventive steps including taking antimalarial medicine and applying insect repellent are advised if you are visiting locations where malaria is prevalent, even if the risk is minimal, particularly in most tourist destinations.

Another illness that tourists may be worried about is yellow fever. However, most tourists do not need the vaccination since there is little danger of yellow fever transmission in Costa Rica proper. The only exception is if you are traveling from a nation where yellow fever is prevalent, such several South American or African nations. In this situation, when entering Costa Rica, you can be asked to provide documentation of your yellow fever vaccine. After only one dosage, the extremely efficient yellow fever vaccination offers lifetime protection.

It's crucial to make sure your regular immunizations are current in addition to these particular ones. This covers vaccinations against influenza, diphtheria, tetanus, and pertussis (DTaP), and measles, mumps, and rubella (MMR). Maintaining your regular vaccines helps protect you and others against outbreaks, even if these illnesses are not very frequent in Costa Rica.

When visiting Costa Rica, there are a number of other health measures to take into account in addition to vaccines. One of the most crucial is to protect oneself from mosquito bites since they may spread illnesses like chikungunya, dengue fever, and the Zika virus. Particularly in lowland regions and during the rainy season, when mosquito numbers are larger, several illnesses are seen in Costa Rica. Wear long sleeves and trousers, apply insect repellent with DEET or another effective component, and stay in accommodations with air conditioning or screens to lower your chance of mosquito bites. Additionally, if you are staying in more modest lodging, mosquito netting may be useful.

Food and water safety are other health considerations. In Costa Rica, tap water is generally safe to drink in the majority of cities and popular tourist locations. To lower the danger of waterborne infections, it is advised to consume bottled or filtered water in more isolated or rural locations. The best course of action when it comes to food is to dine at establishments you can trust and stay away from street food if you are concerned about its safety. Fresh produce should be carefully cleaned, and if you have a sensitive stomach, you should steer clear of raw or undercooked meat and shellfish.

Staying hydrated is essential because of Costa Rica's hot and muggy environment, especially in the lowland and coastal regions. Drink plenty of water and have a reusable bottle with you, particularly if you're going to be trekking or touring outside. Travelers often worry about heat fatigue and dehydration, but these conditions are readily preventable by wearing sunscreen, drinking plenty of water, and taking rests in the shade when necessary.

Being aware of the local fauna when vacationing in Costa Rica is another crucial component of maintaining your health. There are many different kinds of animals in Costa Rica, some of which might be harmful to your health if you don't handle them carefully. For instance, while bites are uncommon, it's vital to be mindful of your surroundings, particularly when trekking in woods or jungles, since several snake species in Costa Rica are poisonous. Because animals may spread illnesses like rabies, it's preferable to watch wildlife from a distance and refrain from touching or feeding them.

It's crucial to make advance plans before visiting Costa Rica if you take regular prescriptions or have any pre-existing medical issues. Bring copies of your prescriptions in case you need a refill, as well as a sufficient amount of any prescription drugs you may need. A simple first aid bag with bandages, antiseptic, painkillers, and any more over-the-counter meds you may need for your vacation is also a smart idea.

It is very advised to get medically comprehensive travel insurance before visiting Costa Rica. Even with the nation's excellent healthcare system, medical crises may still be expensive, particularly for visitors. Travel insurance may provide you peace of mind while you're away by paying for emergency evacuation, medical care, and other unanticipated expenses. Verify that all of the activities you want to engage in, including adventure sports like zip-lining, rafting, and diving, are covered by your insurance policy.

A crucial component of getting ready for a trip to Costa Rica is getting the appropriate immunizations and taking the necessary health measures. You may reduce health risks and travel with confidence if you receive the appropriate vaccinations, protect yourself from insect bites, drink enough of water, and watch what you eat and drink. Being ready with the appropriate health precautions guarantees that your vacation will be both safe and fun, whether you're exploring the rainforests, lounging on the beaches, or learning about Costa Rica's rich culture.

Things to Bring: Packing Essentials

When packing for a vacation to Costa Rica, it's important to take into account the country's varying weather, scenery, and recreational opportunities. Being prepared with the appropriate materials will make your trip more comfortable and pleasurable, whether you're going to the chilly highlands, sun-drenched beaches, or lush rainforests. Knowing what to pack is important for ease, but it's also important to make sure you have everything you need to be secure, comfortable, and ready for anything.

The temperature in Costa Rica is one of the most crucial factors to take into account while packing, since it may vary greatly depending on the area and season. As a tropical nation, Costa Rica has distinct rainy and dry seasons in addition to consistently mild temperatures throughout the year. The dry season, which spans from December to April, is perfect for outdoor activities since it has bright days with low precipitation. However, frequent rain showers, particularly in the afternoons, are a feature of the wet season, which runs from May to November. This might affect what you need to carry.

In order to stay cool and comfortable in the tropical heat, it is imperative that you pack lightweight, breathable clothes. The best options are moisture-wicking textiles, cotton, and linen since they keep you comfortable and dry even in humid environments. Shorts, tank tops, and t-shirts are ideal for daytime clothing, particularly if you're visiting the lowlands or the beach. But it's also a good idea to bring long sleeves and long trousers, which will shield you from the heat, insects, and the colder nights in the highlands.

It is essential to have a high-quality rain jacket or poncho since the weather in Costa Rica may be unpredictable, particularly during the rainy season. For those unexpected downpours, a lightweight, water-resistant jacket that folds up simply and fits in your daypack is perfect. Having rain protection on hand is usually a smart idea since the weather may change suddenly in certain places, even during the dry season.

Footwear is yet another important factor. A pair of comfortable, supportive hiking shoes or boots is essential if you want to engage in any outdoor activities, including hiking. Shoes with enough grip and support are essential since Costa Rica's terrain may be rough and slick, particularly in the hilly and jungle regions. A pair of flip-flops or sandals is helpful for beach days or more relaxed activities. You may need to stroll to see cities or beaches, so make sure your sandals are comfy enough for that.

Because Costa Rica is known for being a paradise for outdoor sports, you should pack the right equipment for the things you wish to accomplish. For instance, it's best to wear loose-fitting, comfortable clothing that doesn't restrict your range of motion if you're zip-lining. To protect yourself from the heat and prevent chafing, think about packing a swim shirt or rash guard for water-based sports like kayaking, surfing, or snorkeling. A swimsuit is essential if you want to spend time near hot springs or waterfalls. It's a good idea to have a swimsuit on available for those impromptu dips, even if swimming isn't your primary activity.

In Costa Rica, where the sun's rays may be quite strong, particularly in lowland and coastal regions, sun protection is crucial. You must wear a baseball cap or a wide-brimmed hat to shield your face and neck from the sun. It's also crucial to wear sunglasses with UV protection to protect your eyes from the intense sunshine. For protection against sunburn, remember to bring lots of sunscreen with a high SPF (at least 30 is advised). It is especially helpful to wear waterproof sunscreen if you will be in and out of the water.

Another essential item is insect repellent, particularly if you plan to spend time in rainforests or other places where mosquitoes are prevalent. It's crucial to take measures since mosquitoes in Costa Rica may spread illnesses including chikungunya, dengue fever, and the Zika virus. It is advised to use repellents using DEET, picaridin, or other potent chemicals. If you're staying in an area where mosquitoes are common, you can also think about packing mosquito coils or a portable insect repellent device.

For day trips and outings, a compact, lightweight daypack is priceless for transporting your necessities. A daypack enables you to easily carry things like your rain jacket, sunscreen, water bottle, food, and camera, whether you're hiking through a national park, touring a town, or spending the day at the beach. To safeguard your stuff in the event of an unexpected downpour, look for a daypack that is waterproof or has a rain cover.

It's crucial to drink enough of water, particularly in Costa Rica's hot and muggy environment. In addition to being good for the environment, carrying a reusable water bottle guarantees that you will always have access to water. Refilling your bottle at your hotel or other clean water sources is possible in many places of Costa Rica. To guarantee the safety of the water you consume while visiting more isolated locations, think about packing a portable water filter or purification tablets.

You should pack a few necessities when it comes to gadgets. A high-quality camera or smartphone is essential for photographing Costa Rica's breathtaking scenery and fauna. Don't forget to include additional memory cards, chargers, and any other necessary supplies. A portable power bank may help you keep your electronics charged while you're going to far-flung locations without access to electrical outlets. Depending on your itinerary, you may also want to pack a waterproof case for your camera or phone, particularly if you want to engage in water sports.

If you're coming from a nation with a different electrical system, you'll need to carry a power adaptor since Costa Rica utilizes the same electrical outlets and voltage (110V) as the US. If you need to charge more than one gadget, it's also a good idea to pack a multi-port USB charger or a tiny power strip since hotel rooms may not have enough outlets.

Things related to health and safety should also be taken into account. Bring a basic first aid kit with band-aids, antiseptic wipes, pain remedies, and any over-the-counter medicines you may require, including motion sickness or anti-diarrheal tablets, in addition to any prescription drugs you use on a regular basis. Additionally helpful for preserving hygiene, particularly while you're on the road, are hand sanitizer and disinfecting wipes.

Don't forget to include an additional pair of glasses or contact lenses, as well as any necessary cleaning tools or solutions. If you notice that your eyes are becoming irritated, think about packing additional solutions or perhaps switching to glasses since the tropical temperature may be harsh on contact lenses.

Naturally, one of the most crucial items to pack is your travel paperwork. Your passport must be valid for at least six months after the day you want to leave Costa Rica. Making photocopies of your passport, visa, and other crucial papers, such as your driver's license, credit cards, and travel insurance policy, is also a smart idea. In the event that they are lost or stolen, keep these duplicates somewhere else from the originals. Digital versions that are safely kept online might also be useful.

It is strongly advised to get travel insurance before visiting Costa Rica. Even though the nation has excellent medical services and is typically safe, unforeseen circumstances like sickness, accidents, or delays in travel might occur. Verify that your insurance covers emergency evacuation, medical costs, and any planned activities, such adventure sports.

Last but not least, think about packing some US dollars, which are often accepted in Costa Rica, particularly in tourist destinations. Even though credit cards are also widely used, it's helpful to have some cash on hand for gratuities, little transactions, and situations when cards may not be accepted. To prevent any problems using your credit or debit cards overseas, it's also a good idea to let your bank know about your trip schedule.

Although packing for Costa Rica involves careful preparation, having everything you need will make your vacation more comfortable, secure, and pleasurable. You may make the most of your trip to this stunning and varied nation by packing the appropriate clothes, equipment, and necessities and taking into account the activities, climate, and any health hazards.

Currency, Language, and Local Etiquette

To properly appreciate and enjoy your vacation to Costa Rica, it is crucial to prepare ahead and be aware of the local currency, language, and cultural customs. These facets of

Costa Rican everyday life have a big impact on how you engage with people, get through various events, and make the most of your stay in this dynamic and varied nation.

First, the Costa Rican colón, which is sometimes shortened to CRC or simply called colones in the plural, is the country's official currency. The Spanish name for the colonón is Cristóbal Colón, in honor of Christopher Columbus. The sign for the money is ₡. Banknotes are available in a range of denominations, usually from 1,000 to 50,000 colones, although coins with lesser values, such 5, 10, 25, 50, 100, and 500 colones, are often used. Since the colón is the most often used method of payment in the nation, it is crucial that you comprehend and get acquainted with it.

Although many regions of Costa Rica, especially tourist destinations, take U.S. dollars, it's still a good idea to have some local money on hand for minor transactions or for visiting more isolated places where dollars may not be accepted. Since costs may be rounded up when paying in dollars, using colones may also be more economical. Airports, banks, and certain hotels provide currency exchange services, but to be sure you're receiving a decent bargain, it's a good idea to check rates and costs. Numerous ATMs may be found in cities and villages, and although they mostly dispense colones, some also allow users to withdraw US dollars. Make sure the ATM is in a well-lit, secure location before using it, and inquire with your bank about any costs associated with making withdrawals from overseas.

Credit and debit cards are often accepted for payments, particularly at lodging facilities, dining establishments, and retail stores in well-known tourist locations. Although American Express is also accepted in select locations, Visa and MasterCard are the most widely used credit cards. Nonetheless, it's still advisable to have some cash on hand since card payments can not be accepted at smaller establishments, local markets, or in rural locations. Tipping is appreciated but not required in Costa Rica. Although a 10% service charge is often included in the bill when dining at a restaurant, you are welcome to tip extra if you thought the service was really good. Tipping for other services, such tour guides or hotel employees, is up to you and usually ranges from a few dollars to a larger sum, depending on the quality of the service.

Let's talk about language. The majority of people in Costa Rica speak Spanish, which is the country's official language. Although most people in tourist destinations speak and understand English, especially those in the hospitality sector, knowing a few simple Spanish phrases may make your trip much more enjoyable and allow you to engage with the local way of life on a deeper level. Ticos, or Costa Ricans, often enjoy it when tourists try to communicate in their native tongue, even if it's merely to say hello or "thank you." Sayings like "Hola" (Hello), "Buenos días" (Good morning), "Gracias" (Thank you), and "Por favor" (Please) may greatly improve the politeness and pleasantness of your interactions.

Knowing a little Spanish will be especially useful if you are visiting more remote or less visited places, since English competence may be low there. The clean and comparatively slow pronunciation of Costa Rican Spanish makes it easy for non-native speakers to comprehend. It might be entertaining to study the distinctive language and idioms used by Ticos, nevertheless. For instance, the popular expression "Pura Vida" captures the essence of Costa Rican culture. The phrase, which literally translates to "pure life," may be used to say hello, good-bye, or that everything is going well. Knowing and using this expression can help you fit in and demonstrate your appreciation for the local way of life.

Regarding cultural etiquette, Costa Rica is renowned for its laid-back and kind vibe. In general, Ticos are kind, courteous, and hospitable to guests; it's crucial to return the favor by acting with decency and consideration at all times. Costa Ricans place a high value on greetings, and it's common to shake hands or give someone a warm wave. A gentle peck on the cheek is customary in more casual contexts, especially between ladies or between a man and a woman. This is not a romantic gesture; rather, it is a show of warmth and kindness.

Talking about delicate subjects like politics or drawing unfavorable parallels between Costa Rica and other nations is best avoided while interacting with natives. Ticos have great pride in their nation's accomplishments, especially its dedication to democracy, peace, and environmental preservation. You may develop positive connections with individuals you meet by speaking with them in an upbeat and receptive manner.

Another important component of Costa Rican culture is respect for the environment. Ticos are proud of their natural heritage, and the nation is a worldwide pioneer in environmental protection. Respecting this as a tourist requires observing responsible travel guidelines, which include refraining from littering, sticking to national park pathways, and paying attention to animals. Both residents and tourists place a high value on maintaining Costa Rica's natural beauty, since its national parks and protected regions are among the most biodiverse in the world.

Costa Ricans tend to dress casually, particularly in rural and seaside communities. Most occasions call for casual, light attire, but if you're traveling to a city or attending a more formal event, it's a good idea to dress a little more formally. Even casual clothing should be maintained tidy since Costa Ricans value neatness and cleanliness. It is considered respectful to wear modest clothes that covers your knees and shoulders while you are in a place of worship, such a church.

Being on time is another crucial component of local etiquette. Being on time for tours, reservations, and other planned events is still crucial, particularly in more formal or professional situations, even though Costa Ricans are typically laid back about time and "Tico time" often alludes to a more flexible attitude to timeliness. A brief phone contact or message informing the other person of your impending tardiness is appreciated.

Costa Ricans are often at ease with intimate touch, particularly amongst friends and family, when it comes to personal space. But it's crucial to respect other people's personal space, especially in more formal situations or when interacting with strangers. It's common practice to show thanks by bringing a little gift, like flowers or a bottle of wine, when you visit someone's house. Make sure to praise the cuisine and express gratitude to your hosts for their hospitality if you are asked to join them for dinner.

CHAPTER 3

GETTING THERE AND AROUND

Flight Options and Major Airports

Being aware of the main airports in Costa Rica and the airline choices available is crucial for a seamless and effective vacation planning process. Costa Rica's colorful culture, breathtaking scenery, and abundant wildlife make it a favorite travel destination for people from all over the globe. Travelers from almost anywhere in the world may now reach the nation because to the wide range of local and international aircraft that service it.

Juan Santamaría International Airport, situated in Alajuela, just outside of San José, Costa Rica, is the main entry point for visitors from outside. The busiest and most significant airport in the nation is this one, which is often referred to by its code SJO. It is well-equipped to manage a high passenger traffic and acts as the primary hub for both local and international flights. A variety of facilities and services are available at Juan Santamaría International Airport to ensure your arrival and departure are as pleasant as possible. In addition to a wide range of shops, eateries, and duty-free shops, you can also find vehicle rental services, money exchange, and ways to go about Costa Rica.

Direct flights to Juan Santamaría International Airport are offered by several major airlines from places in North America, Europe, and Latin America. There are several direct flight alternatives available to passengers from the United States, including major cities like Miami, Los Angeles, New York, Houston, Atlanta, and Dallas. Well-known airlines including American Airlines, Delta Air Lines, United Airlines, and Southwest Airlines operate these routes, offering regular and practical connections. Additionally, direct flights are offered from Canadian cities like Toronto and Montreal, with frequent service provided by carriers like Air Canada and WestJet.

Direct flights from European cities including Madrid, London, and Frankfurt to Costa Rica are available. Travelers from Europe can visit Costa Rica with relative ease because to airlines like Iberia, British Airways, and Lufthansa that provide direct service to San José. Costa Rica is also well-connected within the area, with direct flights available from nations like Mexico, Panama, Colombia, and Brazil for visitors from other regions of Latin America.

Apart from the direct flights to San José, Daniel Oduber Quirós International Airport, Costa Rica's second main international airport, situated in Liberia, Guanacaste, is another important tourist entrance point. Known by its code LIR, this airport provides easy access to the well-liked Guanacaste area, which is renowned for its stunning beaches, upscale resorts, and national parks. With its recent expansion, Daniel Oduber Quirós International Airport currently serves a variety of flights from key locations in North America and Europe.

Numerous airlines, including American Airlines, Delta Air Lines, United Airlines, and WestJet, provide direct flights to Liberia for passengers from the US and Canada. Since the airport's location makes it simple to get to places like Tamarindo, Playa Flamingo, and the Papagayo Peninsula, these flights are especially well-liked among travelers going to the Pacific coast. With direct flights to Liberia from major cities like London and Frankfurt, Liberia is becoming a more and more popular destination for European tourists wishing to visit the northwest region of Costa Rica.

The most convenient airport for your travel arrangements should be taken into account when booking your trip to Costa Rica. Flying into Juan Santamaría International Airport is the most convenient choice if you want to spend the most of your time in the central region of the country, visiting locations like San José, Arenal, or Monteverde. However, flying into Daniel Oduber Quirós International Airport can save you time and simplify your trip if you are interested in the beaches and national parks of the Guanacaste area.

Costa Rica has a number of smaller regional airports that service domestic flights in addition to the main international airports. Travelers may more easily visit areas that would otherwise require lengthy drives or challenging terrain thanks to these airports, which provide access to some of the most isolated and inaccessible regions of the nation. Among the major regional airports are Puerto Jiménez Airport, which offers access to the Osa Peninsula and Corcovado National Park; Quepos Airport, which serves the Manuel Antonio region; and Tamarindo Airport, which serves the well-known beach resort of Tamarindo.

A few local airlines, such as Sansa Airlines and Nature Air, conduct domestic flights inside Costa Rica. These airlines provide frequent service to several regional airports around the nation, making it easy and fast to travel between various regions. In Costa Rica, flying domestically might be particularly beneficial if you're pressed for time and want to make the most of your trip by cutting down on the amount of time you spend traveling between locations.

The schedule of your arrival and departure should also be taken into account while organizing your flight. The geography of Costa Rica is varied, and depending on where you are, the time it takes to go from the airport to your ultimate destination might vary significantly. Particularly if you're traveling to a more isolated location, you may want to think about spending the night near the airport before continuing your trip the following day. On the other hand, sleeping near the airport the night before might help you avoid stress and guarantee that you get to your flight on time if you have an early morning departure.

It is advised to book flights to Costa Rica well in advance, especially during popular vacation times like the dry season (December to April) and significant holidays. There is a notable surge in tourists during these times, which may result in increased prices and restricted availability on well-traveled routes. You can guarantee that you obtain the flight schedule that best suits your trip plans and get lower tickets by making your reservation early.

Travelers from all over the globe may easily reach Costa Rica because to the abundance of local and international airline choices. You can arrange a more effective and pleasurable journey if you are aware of the main airports and the aircraft routes that are accessible. Knowing your alternatives can help you make the best decisions for your trip, whether you're flying into San José or Liberia or taking a local flight to a more isolated area of the nation. Your trip to Costa Rica will go smoothly and stress-free if you prepare beforehand, freeing you up to appreciate all this stunning nation has to offer.

Transportation Within Costa Rica: Public Transport, Car Rentals, and More

Planning a seamless and pleasurable vacation to Costa Rica requires knowing the many forms of transportation that are offered there. Whether you want convenience, affordable alternatives, or the flexibility to see the country at your own speed, Costa Rica has a range of transportation options to suit all kinds of tourists. Knowing how to navigate Costa Rica can make your trip much more enjoyable, whether you want to use public transportation, hire a vehicle, or use another option.

In Costa Rica, public transportation is a must for anybody traveling on a tight budget or who want to fully immerse themselves in the local way of life. The bus system, which links almost every region of Costa Rica—from large cities to small towns and rural areas—is the foundation of the nation's public transportation network. Both residents and visitors utilize buses extensively since they are the most economical mode of transportation. Numerous firms run routes across the nation, making up the vast bus network. However, since there is no central timetable and bus stops can not always be well signposted, the system might be a little confusing for first-time tourists.

The bus terminals in San José, the nation's capital, are dispersed across the city, each of which serves a distinct district. This implies that if you need to switch buses, you may have to go between terminals. In spite of this, buses remain a dependable and affordable means to travel throughout the nation. The buses vary from more basic vehicles for local routes to more contemporary, luxurious coaches for long-distance travel. When traveling between large cities like San José, Liberia, and coastal villages, long-distance buses are a wonderful choice since they usually feature air conditioning and comfortable seats.

It's crucial to have patience and scheduling flexibility if you want to use the bus system. Because of the country's rugged landscape and winding roads, buses may not always arrive on time, and journey durations may be longer than anticipated.

But the travel itself is part of the thrill since the landscape along the route is often beautiful. Local buses are a convenient and affordable choice for quick excursions inside cities or between neighboring villages, however they may become packed during rush hour.

Renting a vehicle is a great way for those who want more freedom and flexibility to see Costa Rica. You may explore off-the-beaten-path locations, drive at your own speed, and take in the breathtaking scenery of the nation without being constrained by public transportation timetables when you rent a vehicle. Both domestic and foreign brands are part of Costa Rica's extensive network of vehicle rental providers. Major airports, cities, and well-known tourist destinations all provide automobile rentals.

It's crucial to choose the appropriate vehicle type for your trip plans when thinking about renting a car in Costa Rica. A typical sedan or small automobile should be enough if you want to remain in cities or drive on well-paved roads.

However, renting a four-wheel-drive (4WD) car is strongly advised if your schedule involves traveling to rural regions, national parks, or coastal spots where the roads may be uneven and unpaved. With their steep slopes, gravel surfaces, and sporadic river crossings, many of Costa Rica's roads may be difficult to navigate, especially in more isolated regions. Better grip and control are provided by a 4WD vehicle, which makes navigating in severe situations safer and more enjoyable.

In Costa Rica, driving can be an experience in and of itself. Secondary roads might vary greatly in quality, even if the major highways are usually in excellent shape. Road conditions might vary rapidly owing to weather, particularly during the rainy season, and there may not be enough signage. Driving carefully and being ready for unforeseen hazards like potholes, sudden turns, or animals crossing the road are crucial. Although Costa Rican drivers are usually polite and tolerant, it's important to be on your guard since their driving might be more aggressive than what some tourists are accustomed to.

Insurance is another factor to take into account while renting a vehicle in Costa Rica. Although basic insurance is sometimes included in the rental fee, further coverage could be required for peace of mind, and car rental insurance in Costa Rica can be costly. Before buying extra insurance from the rental business, it's a good idea to find out whether your credit card company or travel insurance provider offers rental vehicle insurance coverage. Verify the rental agreement's terms and conditions, such as mileage restrictions, fuel rules, and any extra driving costs.

There are various practical modes of transportation for those who would rather not drive alone. Tourists often use shuttle services because they provide door-to-door transportation between important locations. Although shuttles cost more than public buses, they are quicker, more pleasant, and often include hotel pickup and drop-off. You may reserve shuttle services in advance via online platforms, travel companies, or hotels, and they run on set timetables. While private shuttles provide more privacy and flexibility for families or larger parties, shared shuttles are a more affordable choice for single travelers or small groups.

Another way to travel about Costa Rica is via taxi, especially for quick visits inside towns or to neighboring sites. Although most Costa Rican taxis are metered, it's a good idea to make sure the meter is running or settle on a fee before you set off. Official taxis are red with a yellow triangle on the door. It is advised to haggle over the fee in advance since taxis in certain remote regions may not have meters. In some regions of Costa Rica, such as San José and the neighboring areas, ride-sharing services like Uber are also available as an alternative to conventional taxis.

Hiring a private driver or guide is a fantastic choice for those who want an even more individualized experience. You may hire a driver to drive you throughout the nation in a luxurious car via the many private transportation services offered by businesses and individual operators. For anyone who would rather relax and take in the beauty without having to worry about navigating new roads, this is the best choice. A private driver may also serve as a guide, offering advice and local knowledge as you go. Although this service is usually more costly than other modes of transportation, it provides the greatest degree of personalization and convenience.

Boats and ferries are a major form of transportation in

various parts of Costa Rica, especially those that are isolated and near the coast. For instance, to go to well-known locations like Montezuma or Santa Teresa while on the Nicoya Peninsula, you may take a boat from Puntarenas. In places like Tortuguero, where boats are the main means of transportation along the canals and rivers, boat cruises and water taxis are also often used. These water-based modes of transportation are essential for travel in certain regions of Costa Rica and provide a unique way to take in the natural beauty of the nation.

Domestic flights may be a practical means of transportation for larger distances inside Costa Rica. Local airlines like Sansa Airlines and Nature Air service Costa Rica's many rural airports. If you want to cut down on the amount of time you spend traveling between far-flung places, like Liberia and the Caribbean coast or San José and the Osa Peninsula, domestic flights are an excellent choice. The flights provide breathtaking aerial views of the nation's surroundings and are often just an hour long. Plan appropriately, however, since domestic flights are more costly than other modes of transportation and luggage limits could be restricted.

There are many choices for transportation in Costa Rica to accommodate various travel preferences and price ranges. Knowing the country's transportation system can help you travel across Costa Rica with confidence, whether you decide to use the public bus, rent a vehicle for more flexibility, or use shuttles, taxis, or private drivers. You may maximize your time in this stunning and varied nation by choosing the kind of transportation that best suits your requirements, since each one has special benefits of its own. Traveling across Costa Rica may be just as exciting as the actual locations if you prepare beforehand.

CHAPTER 4

TOP ATTRACTIONS AND SIGHTSEEING WONDERS

Arenal Volcano National Park

One of Costa Rica's most famous tourist sites is Arenal Volcano National Park, which draws visitors from all over the globe with its distinctive fusion of adventure and scenic beauty. The magnificent Arenal Volcano, one of the most active volcanoes in Central America until its recent slumber, is located in this national park in the northern portion of the country, close to the town of La Fortuna. The park is a must-visit for thrill-seekers and environment enthusiasts alike because of its diverse ecosystems, vast lava fields, and lush rainforests, which are home to an amazing diversity of animals.

The Arenal Volcano itself is, of course, the focal point of Arenal Volcano National Park. The volcano, which rises to a height of 1,633 meters (5,358 feet), dominates the area with its symmetrical cone form. The Arenal Volcano was the most active in Costa Rica for a long time. It often emitted ash, smoke, and lava, producing a breathtaking natural display. The volcano is still a striking geological feature and a popular destination for park visitors, even though it has been in a resting phase since 2010.

The chance to explore the many landscapes around the volcano is one of the primary attractions of Arenal Volcano National Park. With a total size of around 12,080 hectares (29,850 acres), the park has a variety of ecosystems, ranging from wide savannas to deep rainforests. With hundreds of plant, animal, and bird species flourishing inside its borders, the park is a sanctuary for biodiversity due to its variety of habitats. Wildlife enthusiasts may see a broad diversity of animals in Arenal, including coatis, sloths, howler monkeys, and several bird species like parrots and toucans.

One of the most well-liked activities in Arenal Volcano National Park is hiking, and the park has many well-kept paths suitable for hikers of all skill and fitness levels. From the vast spaces of ancient lava flows to the thick underbrush of the rainforest, these pathways transport tourists through a range of environments. The Sendero Coladas path, which leads to a lava field formed by an eruption in 1992, is one of the most well-traveled routes. Here, visitors may take in expansive views of the volcano and the surrounding area while walking on the hardened lava. The stark contrast between the forest's lush foliage and the black, rocky lava serves as a reminder of the strong natural forces that have molded this area.

The Las Heliconias walk, which meanders through the jungle and provides a more shady, cooler setting, is another well-liked walk. This route offers a chance to see some of the smaller fauna that lives on the forest floor and is perfect for bird viewing. You may see vibrant butterflies flitting by or hear howler monkey sounds resonating through the woods as you go. Every trek provides something new to discover because of the park's tremendous biodiversity, whether it's a secret waterfall, a rare plant species, or the footprints of a wild animal.

In addition to hiking, Arenal Volcano National Park provides a variety of other activities for those looking for more adventure. Visitors may unwind in naturally occurring hot springs heated by the volcano's subterranean lava in the park's surrounding region, which is well-known for its geothermal activity. With several resorts and spas providing access to thermal pools surrounded by verdant gardens and forests, these hot springs are dispersed across the area. In addition to being a soothing activity, soaking in these mineral-rich waters is said to offer medicinal advantages, reviving the body and relieving tense muscles.

Zip-lining is another popular activity in the park and its environs. A number of businesses provide canopy tours, which let you fly through the trees and take in breath-taking views of the volcano and the forest below. Experience the excitement of being hung far above the earth and the rush of wind as you fly over the canopy when zip-lining in Arenal. A unique view on the rainforest and its inhabitants is offered by the canopy tours, which usually consist of a number of platforms and cables, some of which extend over significant distances.

White-water rafting is another well-liked adventure sport in

Arenal. With rapids ranging from Class II to Class IV, the rivers that traverse the area, such the Sarapiquí and the Balsa, provide ideal rafting conditions. The excitement of negotiating these swift-moving waterways while surrounded by thick vegetation is an experience that will never be forgotten, regardless of your level of expertise. Rafting excursions often provide the chance to bathe in the crystal-clear, refreshing waterways and see animals along the riverbanks.

Horseback riding is an additional means of exploring the park and its environs for those who would rather remain on land. You can see the volcano, the lake, and the surrounding area while riding a horse on a guided tour. An delightful and tranquil way to take in Arenal's natural splendor is to ride around this charming area, which is framed by the volcano.

Those who are interested in geology and the study of volcanic activity may also visit Arenal Volcano National Park. The park serves as a living classroom for learning about the forces that mold our world. A rare chance to see and learn about volcanic activity is provided by the mix of more recent lava flows with active geological features like fumaroles and hot springs. Visitors may learn about the volcano's past, the many eruptions it has caused, and the continuous monitoring activities that aid scientists in comprehending and forecasting the behavior of volcanoes.

The biggest lake in Costa Rica, Lake Arenal, is located in the Arenal area, which also has other natural features. A significant source of electricity for the nation, this artificial lake was formed in 1979 as part of a hydropower project. In addition, the lake is a well-liked location for water activities including fishing, windsurfing, and kayaking. In addition to being one of the greatest places in Central America for windsurfing, Lake Arenal's tranquil waters are ideal for a leisurely paddle.

The primary destination for tourists in the region is the town of La Fortuna, which lies close to the Arenal Volcano National Park entrance. In addition to a variety of eateries, retail establishments, and tour companies, La Fortuna has lodging options ranging from affordable hostels to opulent resorts. The town is a great starting point for seeing the park and the neighboring attractions because of its laid-back and friendly vibe. To take advantage of all Arenal has to offer, many tourists decide to stay for a few days.

Arenal Volcano National Park is a place for rest and introspection in addition to excitement and discovery. A special setting where guests may rediscover nature and find peace and quiet is created by the mix of the breathtaking volcanic terrain, the verdant jungle, and the peaceful hot springs. Arenal provides a rejuvenating and restorative experience, whether you want to hike through the forest, swim in a hot pool, or just sit quietly and take in the sounds of the rainforest.

Offering the ideal fusion of adventure, nature, and leisure, Arenal Volcano National Park is one of Costa Rica's most popular tourist destinations. The park offers something for every kind of visitor with its breathtaking scenery, varied fauna, and extensive array of activities. Arenal offers everything you could possibly desire, whether you're searching for excitement, a chance to get in touch with nature, or just a chance to relax in a beautiful environment. In addition to being the highlight of any vacation to Costa Rica, a visit to Arenal Volcano National Park will leave you with enduring memories of the nation's natural treasures and dedication to protecting its distinctive ecosystem.

Manuel Antonio National Park

One of Costa Rica's most prized gems, Manuel Antonio National Park provides tourists with a unique blend of breathtaking beaches and abundant wildlife. This national park, which is located close to the town of Quepos on the Pacific coast, is often recognized as one of the most stunning and biodiverse locations in the nation. With a total size of just 1,983 hectares (4,900 acres), Manuel Antonio is the smallest national park in Costa Rica, but it offers an amazing range of natural beauty and experiences. It is a must-see location for travelers, showcasing Costa Rica's finest attractions.

The beaches of Manuel Antonio National Park are among its main attractions. Some of Costa Rica's most beautiful beaches, with their silky white sand, blue seas, and verdant tropical forest backgrounds, may be found in the park. The park's eponymous beach, Playa Manuel Antonio, is perhaps the most well-known. Visitors may unwind on the sand, swim in the serene waters, or just enjoy the stunning surroundings at this crescent-shaped beach that is encircled by deep vegetation. The surrounding forest offers shelter and a feeling of privacy, and the mild waves make it a great place for swimming, snorkeling, and paddleboarding.

Another beach in the park, Playa Espadilla Sur, has a more wilder vibe but an equally lovely environment. This beach is ideal for anyone seeking a more peaceful experience since it is less busy than Playa Manuel Antonio. Here, surfers and bodyboarders alike are drawn to the somewhat stronger waves. Palm trees and other tropical plants flank the beach, giving a calm setting where guests may peacefully take in the beauty of nature.

Playa Gemelas and Playa Playitas are two of the park's lesser, more isolated beaches in addition to these big ones. For those who are prepared to go beyond the usual routes, these lesser-known hidden treasures provide a more personal encounter. For tourists who like the concept of finding a peaceful place to unwind away from the bigger crowds, these beaches are perfect. These little beaches are unique spots to relax because of their pristine seas and sense of being surrounded by unspoiled nature.

Even while Manuel Antonio's beaches are a big attraction, the park's fauna is just as fascinating. The vast biodiversity of Manuel Antonio National Park is well known, and visitors may see a variety of species in their native environments. More than 350 bird species, 109 mammal species, and a wide variety of reptiles and amphibians may be found in the park. Because of this, it's a photographer's, birdwatcher's, and nature lover's dream come true.

The three-toed sloth is among the most recognizable creatures in Manuel Antonio. These sluggish animals are often seen relaxing in the trees, where they blend in with the thick undergrowth. Many people consider seeing a sloth to be their favorite part of the trip, and park guides are adept at pointing them out, often to the joy of those who may have missed them otherwise. The sloth is a representation of the park's peaceful atmosphere because to its laid-back manner and distinctive look.

In Manuel Antonio, monkeys are yet another popular attraction. Three monkey species may be found in the park: the endangered squirrel monkey, the howler monkey, and the white-faced capuchin. Perhaps the most noticeable are the white-faced capuchins, who are often seen playing in the trees or sometimes approaching tourists in need of food. Although it's fun to observe these monkeys, visitors should keep in mind that human food may be bad for animals, so they shouldn't be fed. Because of their loud, characteristic sounds that reverberate across the jungle, howler monkeys are often heard before they are seen. These noises contribute significantly to the park's natural atmosphere and serve as a reminder of the abundant wildlife all around guests.

One of the park's most beloved residents is the endangered squirrel monkey, sometimes referred to locally as the mono tití. It is a smaller and less common sight. The sight of one of these little monkeys in the wild is a unique experience for every visitor, and efforts have been undertaken to preserve and protect this species. The park's significance as a refuge for endangered species is shown by the existence of these monkeys.

In addition to the animals, Manuel Antonio is a haven for birdwatchers. Numerous bird species, including the elusive resplendent quetzal and beautiful toucans and parrots, are supported by the park's varied habitats. The park's sensory experience is enhanced by the birds' diverse sounds and vivid hues. To capture the splendor of these avian residents, those who are very interested in birdwatching often carry binoculars and long-lens cameras.

Manuel Antonio is also home to a large number of amphibians and reptiles. The park is home to a variety of lizard species, such as the remarkable emerald basilisk, which is known as the "Jesus Christ lizard" since it is often seen sprinting over water. Along the park's pathways, visitors may also see a variety of frog species, including the well-known red-eyed tree frog and others with vivid colors. These amphibians serve as a reminder of the variety and abundance of living forms that flourish in the tropical climates of Costa Rica.

The well-kept pathways in Manuel Antonio National Park provide visitors the opportunity to see the park's many environments, which range from deep rainforests to vantage places along the shore. The main route, which is accessible to most tourists, including those with mobility issues, links the park's entrance to its principal beaches and is comparatively level and simple to walk. This walk is often where tourists first see animals and offers a great introduction to the park's natural splendor.

A number of other routes go further into the park for those seeking a little more adventure. The park's habitats, such as mangroves, rocky outcrops, and expansive vistas of the Pacific Ocean, may all be seen from these routes. For instance, the Punta Catedral walk leads to a picturesque vantage point where guests may take in breath-taking views of the surrounding coastline and ocean. Although this path has some steeper parts and is a little more difficult, the payoff is well worth the effort.

The park's management strategies clearly demonstrate its dedication to conservation. As a protected area, Manuel Antonio National Park works to conserve its animals and ecosystems. There are regulations in place to guarantee that the park continues to be a safe and clean habitat for both people and animals, and the daily number of visitors is restricted to lessen the effect on the ecosystem. By taking these steps, the park's natural beauty is preserved and future generations may enjoy it.

The vicinity of Manuel Antonio National Park provides tourists with a variety of conveniences and activities in addition to its natural charms. The neighboring town of Quepos is a bustling center with a range of lodging options, dining options, and retail establishments. There are choices to fit every kind of visitor, whether you're searching for an affordable hostel or an opulent resort with views of the ocean. Numerous tours and activities, like as boat trips, canopy tours, and guided walks, begin in the town.

The seas around Manuel Antonio provide diving and snorkeling possibilities for people who are interested in marine life. Numerous fish species may be found in the coral reefs and rocky outcrops immediately offshore, which makes it an excellent place for underwater exploration. Popular pastimes that provide tourists a new perspective on the park's shoreline and mangrove woods include kayaking and paddleboarding.

Another place to go if you want to unwind is Manuel Antonio National Park. Beautiful beaches, warm waves, and verdant surrounds come together to provide a tranquil setting where guests may relax and take in the beauty of nature. The park provides a tranquil haven from the rush of daily life, whether you decide to spend your day viewing the animals, hiking, or just relaxing on the beach.

A popular destination in Costa Rica, Manuel Antonio National Park provides an unmatched experience of beaches, animals, and scenic splendor. The park caters to a diverse variety of tourists due to its exceptional blend of rich wildlife and breathtaking coastline landscape. Manuel Antonio has something for everyone, whether you're an adventurer, a nature lover, or someone who just wants to unwind in a beautiful environment. Its dedication to conservation, accessibility, and range of activities guarantee that visitors may take in the park's marvels while also contributing to the preservation of its fragile ecosystems. Not only is a visit to Manuel Antonio National Park a highlight of a Costa Rican vacation, but it also embodies the nation's commitment to environmental preservation and its natural beauty.

Monteverde Cloud Forest

Monteverde Cloud Forest is one of Costa Rica's most captivating destinations, celebrated for its unique blend of ecotourism and conservation efforts. Located in the Cordillera de Tilarán mountain range, this cloud forest is a place of mystique and wonder, where the natural world reveals itself in ways that are both subtle and awe-inspiring. It is a top attraction for tourists who seek a deeper connection with nature and an understanding of the delicate balance that sustains such a rich ecosystem. The Monteverde Cloud Forest embodies the essence of what makes Costa Rica a global leader in conservation and sustainable tourism.

The cloud forest is a rare and unique ecosystem, defined by its high elevation, consistent moisture, and cooler temperatures. The name "cloud forest" comes from the frequent cloud cover that blankets the forest, creating an atmosphere that feels almost otherworldly. The clouds are not just a picturesque backdrop but are integral to the forest's health. Moisture from the clouds condenses on the leaves of the trees and plants, providing a constant source of water that sustains the diverse flora and fauna. This high humidity supports a lush, verdant environment where mosses, ferns, and epiphytes thrive, covering nearly every surface with green life.

Monteverde's cloud forest is renowned for its biodiversity. It is home to an astonishing variety of species, many of which are found nowhere else on Earth. The forest supports over 2,500 species of plants, including more than 400 species of orchids, which are particularly abundant in this area. The richness of plant life in Monteverde is due to the complex interplay of climate, elevation, and moisture, which creates a multitude of microhabitats within the forest. These microhabitats provide niches for a wide array of organisms, contributing to the forest's extraordinary diversity.

The wildlife of Monteverde is equally impressive. The cloud forest is a haven for birdwatchers, who flock to the area to catch a glimpse of its avian inhabitants. Over 400 species of birds have been recorded in Monteverde, including the resplendent quetzal, one of the most iconic and sought-after species in Central America. The quetzal, with its vibrant green and red plumage and long, flowing tail feathers, is often considered a symbol of the cloud forest's beauty and biodiversity. Seeing a quetzal in the wild is a highlight for many visitors, and the Monteverde Cloud Forest Reserve is one of the best places in the world to observe this magnificent bird.

In addition to the quetzal, Monteverde is home to a variety of other bird species, including toucans, bellbirds, and hummingbirds. The forest's complex structure, with its dense canopy and understory, provides ideal conditions for these birds to thrive. The continuous supply of nectar from the forest's many flowering plants supports a high population of hummingbirds, making the area a hotspot for those interested in these tiny, fast-moving creatures. Special hummingbird gardens near the reserve entrance allow visitors to observe these birds up close, as they dart from flower to flower, feeding on nectar.

The cloud forest is also inhabited by a range of mammals, reptiles, amphibians, and insects. Among the mammals, visitors might encounter howler monkeys, spider monkeys, and sloths, as well as elusive creatures like the jaguar and ocelot, though these big cats are rarely seen due to their solitary and nocturnal nature. The forest is home to several species of frogs and salamanders, many of which are endemic to the region. The unique climate and constant moisture of the cloud forest create ideal conditions for these amphibians, which are sensitive to environmental changes.

One of the most fascinating aspects of the Monteverde Cloud Forest is its role in conservation. The forest is protected by several reserves, the most famous of which is the Monteverde Cloud Forest Biological Reserve. Established in 1972, this reserve was created to protect the cloud forest from deforestation and to preserve its unique biodiversity. The reserve covers an area of more than 10,500 hectares (26,000 acres) and includes a wide range of altitudes, from 600 meters to over 1,800 meters above sea level. This variation in elevation contributes to the diversity of habitats found within the reserve, each with its own distinct species and ecological characteristics.

Conservation efforts in Monteverde have been driven by both local and international organizations, as well as by the local community, which has a strong commitment to preserving its natural heritage. The Quaker community, which settled in Monteverde in the 1950s, played a significant role in the early conservation efforts, recognizing the importance of the cloud forest for maintaining the area's water supply and overall ecological health. Their efforts, combined with those of other conservationists, led to the establishment of the Monteverde Cloud Forest Reserve, which has since become a model for conservation in Costa Rica and beyond.

Ecotourism plays a crucial role in the conservation of Monteverde. The revenue generated from tourism helps fund the protection and management of the cloud forest, ensuring that it remains a haven for wildlife and a source of wonder for future generations. Visitors to Monteverde are encouraged to engage in sustainable tourism practices, such as staying on designated trails, minimizing waste, and respecting wildlife. The park's guides are trained in environmental education and often share their knowledge about the importance of conservation with visitors, fostering a greater appreciation for the delicate balance that sustains the cloud forest.

Exploring the Monteverde Cloud Forest is an experience like no other. The reserve's network of trails allows visitors to immerse themselves in the forest's enchanting environment. These trails are carefully maintained to minimize their impact on the ecosystem, while still providing access to some of the most beautiful and ecologically significant areas of the forest. Walking through the cloud forest, visitors can expect to encounter a wide variety of plants and animals, each uniquely adapted to the cool, moist conditions.

One of the most popular trails in the Monteverde Cloud Forest Reserve is the Sendero Bosque Nuboso (Cloud Forest Trail), which takes visitors deep into the heart of the forest. This trail offers a chance to see some of the park's most iconic features, including towering strangler figs, massive ferns, and moss-covered trees. The trail is relatively easy to walk and is suitable for most visitors, though the high humidity and cool temperatures can make the experience physically demanding. Along the trail, visitors may also encounter some of the forest's more elusive wildlife, such as the resplendent quetzal or a shy agouti foraging in the underbrush.

Another highlight of the Monteverde Cloud Forest is the suspension bridges that allow visitors to experience the forest from above. These hanging bridges are suspended high above the forest floor, offering a unique perspective on the canopy and the chance to see birds and other wildlife that are typically hidden from view. Walking across these bridges is both thrilling and serene, as you move through the mist and listen to the sounds of the forest all around you. The bridges are designed to be safe and stable, providing a secure way to explore the upper reaches of the forest.

For those seeking a more adventurous experience, zip-lining is available in the Monteverde area. This activity allows visitors to soar through the canopy, experiencing the forest in a way that is both exhilarating and awe-inspiring. Zip-lining in Monteverde is often combined with guided tours that provide insight into the forest's ecology and the importance of conservation. These tours emphasize the need to protect the cloud forest while also allowing visitors to enjoy its beauty in a responsible and sustainable way.

The Monteverde Cloud Forest is also a center for scientific research. The reserve is home to several research stations where scientists study the cloud forest's unique ecosystems, focusing on areas such as climate change, species interactions, and the effects of human activity on the environment. This research is vital for understanding how to protect the cloud forest and its inhabitants in the face of global environmental challenges. Visitors to Monteverde can learn about ongoing research efforts through interpretive exhibits and guided tours, gaining a deeper understanding of the importance of conservation and the role that science plays in preserving the natural world.

In addition to the Monteverde Cloud Forest Reserve, the area is also home to other reserves and protected areas, such as the Santa Elena Cloud Forest Reserve and the Children's Eternal

Rainforest. Each of these reserves offers a slightly different experience, with varying levels of difficulty for hiking and different opportunities for wildlife observation. The Santa Elena Cloud Forest Reserve, for example, is known for its beautiful views of the Arenal Volcano on clear days, while the Children's Eternal Rainforest, the largest private reserve in Costa Rica, is notable for its extensive network of trails and its focus on environmental education.

Monteverde's commitment to conservation extends beyond the forest itself. The local community is deeply involved in sustainable practices, from organic farming to eco-friendly lodging. Many of the accommodations in Monteverde are designed to minimize their environmental impact, using renewable energy, recycling programs, and water conservation measures. Visitors who choose to stay in these eco-friendly lodges are supporting the local economy while also contributing to the preservation of the cloud forest.

The town of Santa Elena, which serves as the gateway to the Monteverde Cloud Forest, is a charming and welcoming place that caters to visitors with a range of accommodations, restaurants, and shops. The town has a laid-back atmosphere, with a focus on sustainability and community. Visitors can enjoy locally sourced food, shop for handmade crafts, and learn more about the region's culture and history. The town is also a hub for tours and activities, with many options for exploring the cloud forest and surrounding areas.

The Monteverde Cloud Forest is a top attraction in Costa Rica that offers a unique combination of ecotourism and conservation. It is a place where visitors can experience the beauty and wonder of one of the world's most diverse ecosystems while also learning about the importance of protecting such environments for future generations. The cloud forest's rich biodiversity, stunning landscapes, and commitment to sustainability make it a must-visit destination for anyone interested in nature and conservation. Whether you are hiking through the Corcovado National Park: The Untamed Wilderness

Corcovado National Park is often described as the crown jewel of Costa Rica's extensive system of national parks. Located on the remote Osa Peninsula, along the country's southwestern coast, Corcovado is one of the most biologically intense places on Earth, offering visitors an unparalleled opportunity to experience untouched wilderness. This vast expanse of tropical rainforest, coastal ecosystems, and diverse wildlife makes Corcovado a must-visit destination for anyone seeking an authentic connection with nature. The park's pristine and untamed environment sets it apart as a top attraction in Costa Rica, providing a truly immersive experience in one of the world's most remarkable ecosystems.

Covering approximately 424 square kilometers (164 square miles), Corcovado National Park is the largest park in Costa Rica and protects about a third of the Osa Peninsula. The park's remote location and challenging accessibility have helped preserve its wilderness, keeping it largely untouched by human development. The diversity of habitats within the park is extraordinary, encompassing lowland rainforests, highland cloud forests, mangrove swamps, coastal lagoons, and sandy beaches. This range of environments supports an astonishing variety of plant and animal species, many of which are rare, endangered, or found only in this region.

One of the most striking aspects of Corcovado is its incredible biodiversity. The park is home to more than 500 species of trees, 140 species of mammals, 400 species of birds, and countless other species of reptiles, amphibians, insects, and marine life. This makes Corcovado one of the most biologically diverse places on the planet, and a haven for wildlife enthusiasts. The park is a vital refuge for many species that are threatened elsewhere, and it plays a crucial role in the conservation of Costa Rica's natural heritage.

Visitors to Corcovado National Park can expect to encounter an abundance of wildlife in its natural habitat. The park is one of the few places in Central America where all four of the country's monkey species can be seen: the howler monkey, spider monkey, white-faced capuchin, and the endangered squirrel monkey. These primates are often heard before they are seen, with the haunting calls of howler monkeys echoing through the forest, or the playful antics of capuchins observed as they swing from tree to tree.

Corcovado is also one of the best places in Costa Rica to see large mammals. The elusive jaguar, the largest predator in the

Americas, roams the dense forests of the park, though sightings are rare due to their solitary and nocturnal nature. Other large mammals that inhabit Corcovado include the puma, ocelot, tapir, and peccary. The Baird's tapir, the largest land mammal in Central America, is a particularly significant resident of the park. Corcovado is considered one of the last strongholds for this species, and seeing one in the wild is a rare and special experience.

The birdlife in Corcovado is equally impressive, with the park being a paradise for birdwatchers. The scarlet macaw, one of the most iconic birds of the region, is frequently seen flying in pairs or groups, their bright red, yellow, and blue feathers standing out against the green backdrop of the forest. Harpy eagles, one of the largest and most powerful birds of prey, also make their home in the park. These magnificent birds are a symbol of the wilderness that Corcovado represents, and their presence indicates the health of the ecosystem. Additionally, the park is home to a wide variety of other bird species, including toucans, parrots, hummingbirds, and woodpeckers, each adding to the rich tapestry of life in this biodiverse sanctuary.

The marine environment surrounding Corcovado is just as diverse as the land-based ecosystems. The coastal waters off the Osa Peninsula are part of the larger Golfo Dulce, a unique marine environment that is one of the few tropical fjords in the world. These waters are a critical habitat for marine life, including dolphins, sea turtles, and various species of whales. Humpback whales migrate to the warm waters of Golfo

Dulce to breed and give birth, making it one of the best places in Costa Rica to observe these majestic creatures. Additionally, the coral reefs and rocky outcrops along the coast provide habitat for a variety of fish and other marine species, making snorkeling and diving in the area a truly rewarding experience.

Corcovado's beaches, such as those at La Leona, Sirena, and San Pedrillo, offer visitors the chance to explore coastal ecosystems and observe the interactions between land and sea. The park's beaches are often deserted, providing a sense of solitude and connection with nature that is increasingly rare in today's world. These beaches are not only beautiful but also serve as nesting sites for several species of sea turtles, including the endangered olive ridley and leatherback turtles. Witnessing a sea turtle laying its eggs or watching hatchlings make their way to the ocean is an unforgettable experience that underscores the importance of protecting these fragile environments.

One of the defining characteristics of Corcovado National Park is its remoteness and the challenges involved in accessing it. Unlike more easily accessible national parks in Costa Rica, Corcovado requires a greater commitment from visitors in terms of time, effort, and physical endurance. The park is only accessible by boat or on foot, and reaching the park's ranger stations often involves a trek through dense forest or along the coastline. This remoteness is part of what makes Corcovado so special; the journey to reach the park is an adventure in itself, and the reward is an experience of true wilderness that few places can offer.

Hiking is the primary way to explore Corcovado National Park, and the trails within the park vary in difficulty and length. Some trails, such as those leading to the Sirena Ranger Station, are long and challenging, requiring a high level of fitness and preparation. These trails take visitors deep into the heart of the park, where the chances of encountering wildlife are greatest. The trail from Los Patos to Sirena, for example, is a multi-day hike that passes through some of the park's most remote and pristine areas, offering a chance to see a wide variety of species in their natural habitat. Hikes are typically guided, as the dense forest and complex trail system make it easy to get lost without expert knowledge.

The Sirena Ranger Station is the main hub for visitors to Corcovado and serves as a base for exploring the surrounding wilderness. It is located near the coast, where the forest meets the sea, and provides basic accommodations for those who wish to stay overnight in the park. The station is an excellent place to observe wildlife, as animals often come close to the station in search of food and water. Early morning and late afternoon are the best times for wildlife viewing, as many species are most active during these cooler hours. From Sirena, visitors can embark on a variety of hikes, each offering a different perspective on the park's diverse ecosystems.

While the focus in Corcovado is undoubtedly on its natural beauty and wildlife, the park also has a significant role in conservation. The establishment of Corcovado National Park in 1975 was a landmark event in Costa Rica's environmental history, representing a commitment to preserving one of the last remaining tracts of lowland tropical rainforest on the Pacific coast of Central America. The park's creation was driven by the recognition that the Osa Peninsula was a biodiversity hotspot, and that protecting it was crucial for the survival of many species. Since its establishment, Corcovado has become a symbol of Costa Rica's dedication to conservation and sustainable tourism.

The park is managed by Costa Rica's National System of Conservation Areas (SINAC), which works to protect the park's natural resources while also promoting sustainable use and ecotourism. Visitor numbers to Corcovado are strictly controlled to minimize the impact on the environment, and permits are required for entry. This helps to ensure that the park's ecosystems remain intact and that wildlife is not disturbed by excessive human presence. The revenue generated from tourism is used to fund conservation efforts, maintain the park's infrastructure, and support the local communities that depend on the park for their livelihoods.

In addition to its role in conservation, Corcovado also serves as a center for scientific research. The park is a living laboratory where scientists from around the world come to study its unique ecosystems and the species that inhabit them. Research conducted in Corcovado has contributed to a greater understanding of tropical ecology, climate change, and the impact of human activity on natural environments. Visitors to the park can often learn about ongoing research efforts through interpretive programs and guided tours, gaining insight into the challenges and successes of conservation in one of the world's most biodiverse regions.

The experience of visiting Corcovado National Park is one of immersion in nature at its most raw and unspoiled. Unlike more developed tourist destinations, Corcovado offers a sense of adventure and discovery, where the focus is on experiencing the wilderness in its purest form. The park's isolation, challenging terrain, and rich biodiversity make it a destination for those who seek a deeper connection with nature and a true understanding of what it means to conserve our planet's most precious ecosystems.

Corcovado National Park is a top attraction in Costa Rica that embodies the essence of untamed wilderness. Its incredible biodiversity, remote location, and commitment to conservation make it a must-visit destination for anyone interested in nature and adventure. The park offers a unique opportunity to experience one of the most biologically intense places on Earth, where the beauty and complexity of the natural world are on full display. Whether you are hiking through its dense forests, observing its diverse wildlife, or simply taking in the stunning landscapes, a visit to Corcovado is an experience that will leave a lasting impression and a deep appreciation for the importance of preserving our planet's wild places.

Tortuguero National Park

Known as "The Land of Turtles" because it serves as a nesting location for several species of sea turtles, Tortuguero National Park is one of Costa Rica's most famous and significant natural regions. Tortuguero is a distant and mostly unexplored area on the country's northeastern Caribbean coast that is distinguished by a system of meandering rivers, verdant jungles, and long beaches. Tourists interested in environment, animal conservation, and visiting one of the world's most biodiverse locations choose the park because of its exceptional blend of varied habitats and abundant species.

"Tortuguero" means "turtle catcher" in Spanish, reflecting the region's strong connection to marine turtles. The main reason Tortuguero National Park was created in 1975 was to safeguard the green sea turtle's breeding habitats. Since then, it has developed into one of the Western Hemisphere's most significant turtle nesting locations. The beaches of Tortuguero are home to leatherback, hawksbill, and sometimes loggerhead turtles in addition to green sea turtles. The park's character and attraction are largely derived from its dedication to the protection of these species.

A unique and remarkable experience may be had by visiting Tortuguero National Park during the turtle nesting season, which normally lasts from July to October for green turtles and from March to June for leatherbacks. Visitors may see the amazing spectacle of sea turtles arriving on shore to deposit their eggs at this time. It is awe-inspiring and

humbling to see a female turtle painstakingly build a nest on the sand, lay her eggs, and then return to the water. It serves as a reminder of the timeless natural cycles that are still present in this sheltered region of the globe.
But turtles aren't the only attraction in Tortuguero National Park.

Tropical rainforests, mangroves, marshes, lagoons, and canals are all part of the park's broad and varied terrain. Because of these various environments, Tortuguero is home to an incredible variety of animals, making it one of Costa Rica's most biodiverse areas. More than 400 bird species, 60 amphibian species, 30 freshwater fish species, and a wide variety of animals, reptiles, and insects may be found in the park. Because of its richness, Tortuguero is a haven for ecologists and animal lovers.

Because Tortuguero is mostly accessible by boat, exploring the park is a unique experience. The primary transit routes through the park are the rivers and canals, which provide tourists an alternative viewpoint of the rainforest and its people. One of the most well-liked ways to experience the park is by taking a guided boat excursion around the canals, which gives visitors the opportunity to witness a variety of species in their natural environments. Since the light is perfect for photography and the animals are at their most active, these boat trips are often offered in the early morning or late afternoon.

You could come across a range of creatures as you stealthily navigate the rivers, including capuchin monkeys hanging through the trees, howler monkeys, and spider monkeys. Sloths may be spotted hanging to trees in the thick foliage along the riverbanks, while iguanas and caimans can be seen lounging in the sun. Freshwater turtles, fish, and the rare manatee call the rivers home, contributing to the variety of species that may be seen while visiting the park.

Another popular attraction in Tortuguero is birdwatching. The park is one of the greatest locations for birding in Costa Rica because of its varied ecosystems, which serve as a sanctuary for a variety of bird species. Tortuguero is home to a wide variety of birds, including kingfishers, herons, parrots, and toucans. Numerous kinds of birds that have adapted to the watery environment may be found in the wetlands and mangroves. Experiences that encapsulate Tortuguero's natural splendor include seeing a vibrant toucan soar above or hearing a parrot's cry reverberate through the jungle.

Visitors to Tortuguero National Park may explore the park's network of paths that meander through the jungle in addition to taking boat cruises. A closer look at the park's rich greenery and diverse species may be had on these routes. From the sounds of birds and monkeys to the aroma of moist dirt and leaves, visitors may fully experience the sights, sounds, and scents of the rainforest while strolling through it. The pathways also provide chances to see some of the forest's smaller and more elusive animals, such insects, lizards, and frogs.

One of the main goals of Tortuguero's administration is the

preservation of its natural resources. A crucial first step in defending the region's distinctive ecosystems from poaching, deforestation, and other human activities endangering its biodiversity was the creation of Tortuguero National Park. In order to guarantee the long-term preservation of the park's fauna and ecosystems, Costa Rica's National System of Conservation Areas (SINAC) now oversees the park. Research and monitoring projects, especially those pertaining to sea turtle populations, help the park's conservation efforts.

Sea turtle nesting and hatching monitoring is one of the main conservation projects in Tortuguero. Data on the number of turtles nesting each season, the success of hatching events, and the difficulties the turtles encounter are gathered by researchers and volunteers. Understanding the condition of the turtle populations and creating conservation plans depend heavily on this data. In order to guarantee that the advantages of ecotourism are distributed and that the local populace is actively involved in preserving their natural heritage, community engagement is also essential in these conservation initiatives.

Another resource for environmental education is Tortuguero National Park. The park educates visitors on the value of preserving the world's rainforests and seas, as well as the part that everyone of us can play in preserving these essential ecosystems. Exhibits and information on the park's species, ecosystems, and conservation initiatives are available in the visitor center. Additional chances to learn about the ecology and difficulties facing the park are offered via guided tours conducted by informed local guides.

The primary entry point for tourists is the town of Tortuguero, which is situated just outside the national park. Despite its modest size, Tortuguero is a thriving town that places a high priority on conservation and ecotourism. The town has a variety of lodging options that are all intended to fit in with the surrounding environment, ranging from affordable lodges to more luxurious eco-resorts. Visitors may support the community's attempts to live in peace with the environment and enjoy the local culture by staying in Tortuguero.

Due to its distant location and lack of road access, Tortuguero National Park needs significant preparation to reach. The majority of tourists go from the village of La Pavona by boat or fly domestically to Tortuguero's little airport. The excursion includes the drive to Tortuguero, which passes through some of Costa Rica's most breathtaking and pristine scenery. One of the highlights is the boat journey to Tortuguero, which provides breathtaking views of the river and the surrounding jungle as you get closer to the park.

After arriving at Tortuguero, guests are free to go around the park at their own speed, whether that means strolling the trails, taking guided excursions, or just lounging on the beaches. In addition to being crucial for sea turtles, the park's beaches provide tourists with a chance to take in the natural splendor of the Caribbean coast. Strong currents make it typically unsafe to swim in the park's waters, but the beaches provide a serene environment for strolling, seeing birds, or just enjoying the scenery.

In Tortuguero National Park, guests may establish a genuine connection with the natural world. The park provides a unique experience that is instructive and motivating because of its isolated location, abundant biodiversity, and conservation emphasis. A trip to Tortuguero offers a chance to experience the marvels of nature and to understand the significance of preserving our planet's most valuable ecosystems, whether you're seeing sea turtles nest on the beach, taking a boat tour of the jungle, or learning about the park's conservation initiatives.

One of Costa Rica's most popular destinations is Tortuguero National Park, which provides a singular and immersive experience in an area that is both biologically important and incredibly beautiful. The park is a must-see because of its dedication to conservation, abundant biodiversity, and function as a refuge for endangered sea turtles. Tortuguero offers an incredible adventure into the heart of Costa Rica's wilderness for individuals who want to see nature in its most pristine state, learn about the delicate balance of ecosystems, and help preserve our planet's natural riches.

San José

Travelers looking to get a sense of the essence of Costa Rica are drawn to San José, the vibrant capital city, which provides a rich tapestry of history and culture. San José stands out as the cultural and historical hub of Costa Rica, where tourists can learn about the country's history, take in its thriving arts scene, and get a taste of the local way of life, despite the country's well-known natural beauty. The city's blend of colonial-era architecture, contemporary urban growth, and a vibrant environment makes it an intriguing setting for learning about Costa Rica's history.

San José was established in the middle of the 18th century, and its history is strongly linked to Costa Rica's growth as a country. In 1737, the city was founded as Villa Nueva, a tiny farming community, to help the Central Valley's expanding agricultural industry. In contrast to many other capitals in Latin America, San José was not constructed during the early colonial era; rather, it developed later as a consequence of the rise of coffee growing, which was essential to the development and prosperity of the city. Coffee was Costa Rica's top export by the early 19th century, and San José was well situated in the Central Valley to facilitate trade and business.

Since Costa Rica declared its independence from Spain in 1821, San José has grown from a little town to the nation's capital. San José progressively emerged as the nation's political and administrative hub after independence, and after a short civil war between Central Valley communities, it was named the country's capital in 1823. With a population of over 300,000 in the city proper and over 2 million in the metropolitan region, San José is now a thriving urban hub thanks to this choice.

Exploring San José's rich architectural legacy, which captures the city's historical development, is one of the main highlights. One of Costa Rica's most recognizable structures, the National Theater was finished in 1897 and serves as a reminder of the late 19th-century artistic ambitions of the nation. Funds from a coffee export tax were used to construct the theater, signifying the significance of the coffee sector to Costa Rica's economic and cultural life. The building's neoclassical design, with its grand façade, marble interiors, and intricate frescoes, showcases the European influences that were popular among the country's elite at the time. Today, the National Theater remains a central venue for cultural performances, including concerts, plays, and ballets, and is a must-visit for anyone interested in Costa Rica's cultural history.

Another important architectural site in San José is the Metropolitan Cathedral, located in the heart of the city. The cathedral, originally constructed in 1802 and later rebuilt after an earthquake in 1821, represents the city's colonial past and its role as a center of religious life in Costa Rica. The cathedral's design combines elements of neoclassical and Baroque styles, with a simple yet elegant exterior and an interior that features stained glass windows, intricate woodwork, and religious art. The cathedral is not only a place of worship but also a symbol of San José's resilience and continuity through periods of change and upheaval.

For those interested in Costa Rica's political history, a visit to the former Bellavista Fortress, now home to the National Museum of Costa Rica, offers valuable insights. The fortress, built in 1917, played a significant role during the country's civil war in 1948, a conflict that ultimately led to the abolition of the military and the establishment of Costa Rica's enduring democracy. The National Museum, housed within the fortress, provides a comprehensive overview of Costa Rica's history, from pre-Columbian times to the present day. The museum's exhibits include archaeological artifacts, colonial-era relics, and displays on Costa Rica's natural history and cultural heritage. Exploring the museum gives visitors a deeper understanding of the events and forces that have shaped the nation.

San José is also a city of parks and public spaces, where the history and culture of Costa Rica are celebrated and preserved. The Central Park, located in front of the Metropolitan Cathedral, is a lively gathering place for both locals and tourists. The park is surrounded by important historical buildings, including the National Theater and the Grand Hotel Costa Rica, and serves as a focal point for public life in the city. The park's atmosphere is vibrant, with street vendors, musicians, and families enjoying the open space, making it a great spot to experience the everyday rhythm of San José.

Nearby, the Morazán Park, with its distinctive metallic dome, known as the Temple of Music, is another notable site. The park is named after Francisco Morazán, a Central American leader who advocated for the unification of the region during the 19th century. The Temple of Music, built in 1920, is an architectural gem inspired by the rotunda of the Palace of Versailles. The park is a popular venue for concerts and cultural events, reflecting the city's commitment to fostering a lively arts scene.

San José's cultural life extends beyond its historical sites to include a thriving arts and entertainment scene. The city is home to numerous museums, galleries, and theaters that showcase both traditional and contemporary Costa Rican art. The Museum of Costa Rican Art, located in the former international airport terminal building, is a prime example of the city's dedication to preserving and promoting the country's artistic heritage. The museum's collection includes works by some of Costa Rica's most renowned artists, as well as temporary exhibitions that highlight the diversity and dynamism of the local art scene.

For a more contemporary cultural experience, visitors can explore the city's many galleries, which feature works by emerging Costa Rican artists. The Amón Cultural Center, situated in the historic Barrio Amón district, is a hub for contemporary art and cultural events. The center hosts exhibitions, workshops, and performances that engage with current social and political issues, offering a space for dialogue and creative expression. Exploring these galleries provides a window into the modern cultural landscape of Costa Rica, where traditional and contemporary influences intersect.

San José's role as the cultural capital of Costa Rica is also evident in its festivals and celebrations. Throughout the year, the city hosts a variety of events that reflect the country's diverse cultural traditions. The International Arts Festival, held every two years, is one of the most significant cultural events in Central America, attracting artists and performers from around the world. The festival features a wide range of activities, including theater, dance, music, and visual arts, and takes place in various venues across the city, transforming San José into a vibrant cultural stage.

Another important celebration is the Festival of Lights, held in December to mark the start of the holiday season. The festival features a grand parade through the city's streets, with elaborate floats, marching bands, and performances that light up the night. The Festival of Lights is a highlight of the year for many Costa Ricans and offers visitors a chance to experience the festive spirit and communal joy that characterize the country's celebrations.

San José is also a culinary destination, where the flavors of Costa Rica's diverse regions come together in a vibrant food scene. The city's markets, such as the Central Market and the Borbón Market, are excellent places to explore local cuisine and experience the hustle and bustle of daily life. The Central Market, in particular, is a sensory experience, with its narrow aisles filled with vendors selling everything from fresh produce and meats to traditional handicrafts and herbal remedies. During their interactions with locals, visitors can sample typical Costa Rican dishes like ceviche (marinated seafood), casado (a plate with rice, beans, meat, and salad), and gallo pinto (a rice and bean dish). They can also learn about the ingredients and culinary traditions that define the country's food culture.

In addition to its traditional cuisine, San José is home to a growing number of innovative restaurants that fuse local ingredients with international influences. The city's culinary scene reflects the broader trends of globalization and cultural exchange, with chefs experimenting with new flavors and techniques while staying rooted in Costa Rican traditions. Dining in San José offers a taste of the country's rich culinary heritage, as well as a glimpse into its evolving food culture.

Beyond its historical and cultural attractions, San José serves as a gateway to the many natural wonders of Costa Rica. The city's central location makes it an ideal base for exploring the country's diverse landscapes, from the cloud forests of Monteverde to the beaches of the Pacific and Caribbean coasts. Day trips from San José allow visitors to experience the natural beauty that Costa Rica is famous for, while still enjoying the conveniences and cultural offerings of the capital.

San José's role as a transportation hub also makes it easy for travelers to explore the rest of the country. The city is well-connected by road and air, with the Juan Santamaría International Airport located just outside the city, providing easy access to both domestic and international destinations. Whether you're planning a short stay in San José or using it as a jumping-off point for further exploration, the city's infrastructure and amenities ensure a comfortable and convenient experience.

San José is a city that offers a rich and immersive experience for tourists interested in exploring Costa Rica's history and culture. From its colonial-era architecture and historical landmarks to its vibrant arts scene and culinary delights, the capital city provides a deep and multifaceted understanding of the country's heritage and contemporary life. San José is not just a place to pass through on the way to Costa Rica's natural attractions; it is a destination in its own right, where the stories of the past and the energy of the present come together to create a unique and memorable experience. For those who seek to understand the heart of Costa Rica, a visit to San José is essential, offering insights and experiences that will enrich your understanding of this remarkable country.

CHAPTER 5

HIDDEN GEMS

Cahuita

Travelers looking to discover Costa Rica's lesser-known locations can find a genuine and pristine experience at Cahuita, a tiny coastal village on the Caribbean coast. Cahuita, which is in the province of Limón, is a great place for people who wish to get away from it all, unwind on immaculate beaches, and learn about the rich Afro-Caribbean culture that characterizes this area. It is tucked away between the Caribbean Sea's turquoise waters and a lush tropical rainforest. Cahuita has maintained its charm and relaxed vibe despite its increasing popularity among tourists, giving it the ideal getaway from the busier tourist destinations.

The village of Cahuita is renowned for its laid-back atmosphere and welcoming residents who have strong ties to the natural world and their cultural history. The local way of life demonstrates how Cahuita has preserved a strong feeling of community and tradition, in contrast to other of Costa Rica's more developed regions. The Afro-Caribbean community that arrived in the town in the 19th century is deeply ingrained in its history and continues to have a significant cultural impact today. The town's distinctive fusion of African, indigenous, and Caribbean elements may be seen in Cahuita's culture, music, food, and language.

The neighboring Cahuita National Park, one of Costa Rica's most stunning and biologically varied protected areas, is one of the city's primary attractions. The park is a sanctuary for both terrestrial and marine species, with around 2,711 hectares of land and 23,290 hectares of maritime space. The park is well known for its breathtaking beaches, lush rainforest, and coral reefs, all of which provide a diverse range of plant and animal life a thriving home. In contrast to many other national parks, Cahuita National Park does not charge an admission fee; instead, visitors are urged to donate to assist the park's conservation initiatives.

Any visitor to the region should make time to see Cahuita National Park. The park has a variety of activities that let guests get up close and personal with its natural splendor. Hiking along the park's well-kept paths, which meander through the rainforest and along the shore, is one of the most well-liked pastimes. Along with offering breathtaking views of the Caribbean Sea, the main route parallels the beach and leads to a number of remote beaches where guests may swim, sunbathe, or just unwind under the palm palms. You'll probably come across a mix of animals as you stroll around the park, such as sloths, raccoons, howler monkeys, and other bird species. In addition to a variety of tropical flora and flowers that contribute to the region's rich biodiversity, the park is home to a number of reptilian and amphibian species.

With its smooth white sand, crystal-clear seas, and swaying coconut trees, Cahuita's beaches are among the most stunning and pristine in all of Costa Rica. One of the most visited beaches in the national park is Playa Blanca, which is well-known for its shallow, serene waters that are ideal for swimming and snorkeling. Numerous marine species, such as sea urchins, colorful fish, and sometimes stingrays and tiny sharks, may be seen on the beach's coral reefs. Since Cahuita's protected reefs provide some of the greatest underwater views in the nation, snorkeling is a popular activity for many tourists. There are snorkeling trips that let guests explore the reefs with a guide who can identify the many species that call the region home.

Cahuita National Park also provides opportunity for marine conservation enthusiasts to learn about coral reef preservation and the efforts being made to maintain these important ecosystems. To reduce their negative effects on the reefs, visitors are urged to conduct safe diving and snorkeling in the park's protected maritime region. Knowledgeable with the marine environment, the park's personnel and local guides can shed light on issues like pollution, overfishing, and climate change that affect coral reefs.

In addition to Cahuita National Park's breathtaking natural surroundings, the town of Cahuita is a delightful destination. The town's main street is dotted with vibrant architecture, little stores, and neighborhood eateries serving authentic Afro-Caribbean cuisine. Cahuita's cuisine, which includes meals made with fresh seafood, coconut milk, and a range of spices, reflects the town's cultural past. Patacones (fried plantains), jerk chicken, and rice and beans cooked in coconut milk are popular meals. The sounds of calypso and reggae music, which often float from nearby taverns and eateries, add to the town's relaxed vibe.

The Afro-Caribbean community's cultural customs may also be experienced at Cahuita. The town celebrates its cultural legacy with a number of festivals and events held throughout the year. The August celebration of the Día de la Cultura Negra (Day of Black Culture), which includes traditional cuisine, dancing, and music, is one of the most significant occasions. Both residents and tourists may learn about the history and contributions of Costa Rica's Afro-Caribbean community during this event. A greater comprehension of the town's cultural character may be gained from the vibrant ambiance and feeling of community that these festivals provide.

Cahuita is the perfect place for those who want to unwind and rest in addition to its natural and cultural attractions. The village is the ideal location to escape the strains of daily life because of its slower pace of life and lovely surroundings. Cahuita provides a tranquil and restorative experience that is difficult to obtain in more popular regions, whether you're strolling around the town, relaxing on the beach, or having a leisurely lunch at a restaurant by the sea.

The surrounding area provides a multitude of chances for adventure and exploration for those wishing to go outside of Cahuita. Another well-liked Caribbean coast attraction is the adjacent town of Puerto Viejo de Talamanca, which is well-known for its lively nightlife, surfing beaches, and thriving cultural scene. Another protected area with great hiking, birding, and animal viewing possibilities is the Gandoca-Manzanillo National animal Refuge, which is situated south of Puerto Viejo. The refuge is a vital location for the survival of several endangered species and is home to a range of ecosystems, such as lowland rainforest, wetlands, and mangroves.

Part of the allure of Cahuita is that, despite its numerous charms, it is still comparatively unexplored. As more visitors become aware of the town's charms, it has been able to maintain its charm and originality. This feeling of being a secret treasure is what makes Cahuita such a unique destination. Visitors may experience an authentic and pristine side of Costa Rica, which is becoming more and more uncommon in today's world, thanks to the town's dedication to conserving its natural and cultural history.

For tourists looking for a genuine experience on Costa Rica's Caribbean coast, Cahuita is a special and worthwhile visit because of its pristine beauty, vibrant culture, and dedication to conservation. Cahuita provides an experience that is both enlightening and memorable, whether you're exploring the immaculate beaches and coral reefs of Cahuita National Park, taking in the town's lively Afro-Caribbean culture, or just taking in the tranquil ambiance of this undiscovered jewel. Cahuita offers a unique chance to engage with the natural environment and the cultural variety that characterizes Costa

Rica for those who want to go beyond the well-traveled tourist routes.

Rio Celeste

Rio Celeste, often referred to as the Turquoise River of Legends, is one of Costa Rica's most enchanting and mysterious natural wonders. Nestled within the lush confines of Tenorio Volcano National Park, this river captivates visitors with its surreal, sky-blue waters that appear almost otherworldly. For those who seek to explore the hidden gems of Costa Rica, Rio Celeste offers a breathtaking experience that combines natural beauty, fascinating geological phenomena, and the rich cultural lore that surrounds this unique location.

The allure of Rio Celeste begins with the striking color of its waters, which are unlike anything found elsewhere in the country. The river's vibrant turquoise hue has long been a source of wonder and speculation, giving rise to various legends and stories. According to local folklore, the river obtained its color when, after painting the sky, God washed His paintbrushes in its waters, leaving behind the brilliant blue that continues to dazzle all who see it. While this tale adds a magical dimension to the experience, the true explanation for the river's color lies in the unique chemical composition of its waters.

The scientific explanation for Rio Celeste's remarkable color is just as fascinating as the legends. The river's blue hue results from a natural phenomenon known as the Mie scattering effect, which occurs when sunlight interacts with the tiny mineral particles suspended in the water. These particles, which consist primarily of aluminum silicates, reflect sunlight in a way that emphasizes the blue portion of the spectrum, giving the river its distinct turquoise appearance. This phenomenon is particularly evident at the point where two smaller rivers, the Río Buenavista and the Quebrada Agria, merge to form the Rio Celeste. Known as "El Tenidero," or "The Dyeing Point," this confluence is where the color transformation occurs, creating a mesmerizing visual effect that leaves visitors in awe.

To fully appreciate the beauty and mystery of Rio Celeste, a visit to Tenorio Volcano National Park is essential. The park, located in the northern part of Costa Rica, near the town of Bijagua, encompasses a diverse range of ecosystems, from dense rainforests to volcanic landscapes. The park's namesake, the Tenorio Volcano, is an inactive stratovolcano that towers over the surrounding terrain, adding to the dramatic scenery. The area is rich in biodiversity, with a variety of plant and animal species that thrive in the park's lush environment.

Hiking to Rio Celeste is one of the most rewarding experiences for visitors to the park. The main trail, known as the "Sendero Misterios del Tenorio," or "Mysteries of Tenorio Trail," is a well-maintained path that takes hikers through the heart of the rainforest, offering glimpses of the region's abundant flora and fauna. The trail is approximately 7 kilometers (4.3 miles) round trip and can be moderately challenging, especially in wet conditions, as the terrain can become muddy and slippery. However, the effort is well worth it, as the trail leads to some of the park's most stunning natural features, including the river, waterfalls, hot springs, and more.

As you hike through the rainforest, the sound of birdsong and the rustling of leaves create a serene atmosphere, immersing you in the sights and sounds of the jungle. Along the way, you may encounter a variety of wildlife, including howler monkeys, sloths, toucans, and colorful frogs. The diversity of plant life is equally impressive, with towering trees, vibrant flowers, and a dense canopy that filters the sunlight, creating a dappled effect on the forest floor. The trail itself is an experience, offering a sense of adventure and discovery as you make your way deeper into the park.

One of the highlights of the hike is reaching the Rio Celeste Waterfall, or "Catarata Rio Celeste." This stunning waterfall is one of the most photographed spots in the park and for good reason. As the river plunges 30 meters (98 feet) into a natural pool below, the brilliant turquoise water contrasts sharply with the surrounding greenery, creating a scene of almost unreal beauty. The waterfall is a powerful reminder of the natural forces at work in the park, as the water cascades down the cliff face with a thunderous roar, sending mist into the air. Visitors can descend a set of stairs to get a closer view of the waterfall and take in the full majesty of this natural wonder.

Continuing along the trail, you'll come to a series of natural hot springs, known as "Las Ollas," or "The Pots." These geothermal pools are heated by the volcanic activity beneath the park and offer a relaxing spot to soak and unwind after the hike. The hot springs are surrounded by lush vegetation, creating a peaceful and rejuvenating environment. The warm waters are rich in minerals and are believed to have therapeutic properties, making them a popular stop for those looking to experience the healing power of nature.

Another fascinating feature of the Rio Celeste area is the "Borbollones," or "Bubbling Pools." This section of the river is characterized by bubbling hot springs that release sulfuric gases, creating a series of small, boiling pools. The sight and sound of the bubbling water add to the otherworldly feel of the area, reminding visitors of the volcanic forces that have shaped the landscape over millennia. The bubbling pools are a striking example of the geothermal activity that continues to influence the region, and they offer a unique insight into the dynamic processes that occur beneath the Earth's surface.

As you near the end of the trail, you'll reach the famous "El Tenidero," where the two rivers merge to form the Rio Celeste. This is where the magic happens, as the clear waters of the Río Buenavista and the mineral-rich waters of the Quebrada Agria combine to create the vibrant turquoise color for which the river is known. Standing at this point, you can observe the precise moment when the water changes color, a phenomenon that has captivated scientists and visitors alike. The confluence of the two rivers is a powerful reminder of the interconnectedness of natural processes and the beauty that can arise from their interaction.

Beyond its natural beauty, Rio Celeste and Tenorio Volcano National Park are also important for their role in conservation. The park is part of Costa Rica's extensive network of protected areas, which are dedicated to preserving the country's unique biodiversity and natural heritage. The conservation efforts in the park are focused on maintaining the health of its ecosystems, protecting endangered species, and promoting sustainable tourism practices. Visitors to the park are encouraged to follow guidelines that help minimize their impact on the environment, such as staying on designated trails, avoiding the use of harmful chemicals, and respecting wildlife.

Rio Celeste is not just a destination for nature lovers and hikers; it is also a place of cultural significance. The legends and stories associated with the river are an integral part of the local folklore, and they reflect the deep connection that the people of the region have with their natural surroundings. The river is seen as a symbol of the power and mystery of nature, and its vibrant color is a reminder of the beauty that can be found in the most unexpected places. For visitors, exploring Rio Celeste offers an opportunity to connect with both the natural and cultural heritage of Costa Rica.

The town of Bijagua, located near the entrance to Tenorio Volcano National Park, serves as the main gateway for visitors to Rio Celeste. Bijagua is a small, rural community that has embraced ecotourism as a way to support its local economy while preserving its natural resources. The town offers a range of accommodations, from rustic lodges to more upscale eco-resorts, all of which are designed to blend in with the natural environment. Staying in Bijagua allows visitors to experience the warm hospitality of the local people and to learn more about the region's traditions and way of life.

In addition to exploring Rio Celeste, visitors to Bijagua can enjoy a variety of other activities, such as birdwatching, horseback riding, and visiting local farms. The area is known for its rich biodiversity, and birdwatchers in particular will find plenty to keep them occupied, with the chance to see species such as the resplendent quetzal, keel-billed toucan, and blue-crowned motmot. Many local guides offer birdwatching tours that provide insights into the region's avian life and the importance of conservation efforts.

For those looking to experience the agricultural traditions of the region, a visit to one of the local farms is a must. Many farms in the area offer tours that allow visitors to learn about sustainable farming practices, coffee production, and the cultivation of tropical fruits and vegetables. These tours provide a deeper understanding of the relationship between the land and the people who live there, as well as the challenges and rewards of farming in such a diverse and dynamic environment.

Rio Celeste, with its stunning turquoise waters, lush rainforest, and fascinating geological phenomena, is truly one of Costa Rica's hidden gems. The river's unique beauty and the legends that surround it make it a must-visit destination for anyone seeking to explore the country's natural wonders. Whether you are drawn by the mystery of the river's color, the allure of the rainforest, or the opportunity to connect with the local culture, Rio Celeste offers an experience that is both enriching and unforgettable. For those who venture off the beaten path to discover this hidden treasure, the rewards are nothing short of magical.

Orosi Valley: A Journey into Costa Rica's Coffee Heartland
The Orosi Valley, nestled in the lush, rolling hills of Costa Rica's Central Valley, is a hidden gem that offers a journey into the heart of the country's coffee-growing tradition. This region, rich in natural beauty and cultural heritage, provides a unique and immersive experience for tourists who seek to explore the roots of Costa Rican coffee culture while enjoying the serene landscapes that have shaped the lives of generations of farmers. The Orosi Valley, with its verdant coffee plantations, colonial architecture, and warm local communities, is a place where time seems to slow down, inviting visitors to savor every moment of their stay.

Located about 35 kilometers southeast of the capital, San José, the Orosi Valley is part of the province of Cartago, an area known for its agricultural productivity and historical significance. The valley is framed by the towering mountains of the Central Highlands, including the majestic Irazú and

Turrialba volcanoes, whose fertile soils and cool climate create the perfect conditions for growing high-quality coffee. The region's natural landscape is characterized by its vibrant greenery, meandering rivers, and mist-covered peaks, offering a picturesque setting that has remained largely untouched by modern development.

The history of the Orosi Valley is deeply intertwined with the history of coffee in Costa Rica. Coffee was introduced to Costa Rica in the late 18th century, and by the early 19th century, it had become the country's most important export crop. The Orosi Valley, with its ideal growing conditions, quickly emerged as one of the primary coffee-producing regions in the country. The success of coffee farming in the valley played a crucial role in the development of Costa Rica's economy and its integration into global trade networks. Today, the Orosi Valley remains one of the country's most important coffee-growing areas, producing beans that are renowned for their quality and flavor.

Exploring the Orosi Valley offers visitors a unique opportunity to experience Costa Rica's coffee culture firsthand. The valley is dotted with coffee plantations, many of which have been owned and operated by the same families for generations. These plantations, or "fincas," are often open to visitors, offering guided tours that provide insights into the coffee production process, from the cultivation of the coffee plants to the harvesting, processing, and roasting of the beans. During these tours, visitors can walk through the coffee fields, learn about the different stages of coffee production, and even participate in some of the activities, such as picking ripe coffee cherries or sorting beans.

One of the highlights of visiting a coffee plantation in the Orosi Valley is the opportunity to taste the coffee that is produced on-site. Many fincas have their own small cafes or tasting rooms, where visitors can sample freshly brewed coffee made from beans grown just steps away. The experience of sipping a cup of coffee while overlooking the fields where it was grown is a memorable one, offering a deeper appreciation for the care and craftsmanship that goes into producing each batch of beans. The rich aroma and complex flavors of the coffee, combined with the tranquil setting of the valley, make this a truly immersive experience.

In addition to its coffee heritage, the Orosi Valley is home to a wealth of cultural and historical attractions. The town of Orosi, which lies at the heart of the valley, is one of the oldest communities in Costa Rica, with a history that dates back to the Spanish colonial period. The town's most famous landmark is the Iglesia de San José de Orosi, a colonial-era church that was built in 1743 by Franciscan missionaries. This church is one of the few remaining structures from the early colonial period in Costa Rica and is considered a national monument. The whitewashed adobe walls and simple, yet elegant, design of the church reflect the architectural style of the time, and its well-preserved interior features original wooden beams, religious paintings, and a collection of sacred artifacts.

The adjacent Museo de Arte Religioso, or Religious Art Museum, is housed in the former monastery that was once part of the church complex. The museum's exhibits include religious art, artifacts, and historical documents that provide a glimpse into the spiritual life of the early settlers in the Orosi Valley. The museum's tranquil courtyard, with its stone fountain and lush gardens, offers a peaceful retreat where visitors can reflect on the rich history and cultural heritage of the region.

The Orosi Valley is also known for its natural beauty, and there are several spots where visitors can enjoy the stunning landscapes that characterize this region. The Mirador de Orosi, or Orosi Lookout, is a popular viewpoint that offers panoramic views of the valley, the Reventazón River, and the surrounding mountains. From this vantage point, visitors can take in the patchwork of coffee plantations, small farms, and dense forests that make up the valley's landscape. The lookout is particularly beautiful at sunrise or sunset when the soft light bathes the valley in a golden glow.

For those who enjoy outdoor activities, the Orosi Valley offers a range of options for exploring the natural environment. The valley is crisscrossed by a network of trails that lead through coffee fields, forests, and along riverbanks, providing opportunities for hiking, birdwatching, and photography. The region's rivers, including the Reventazón and Orosi Rivers, are known for their clear waters and scenic beauty, making them ideal for activities such as fishing, kayaking, or simply enjoying a peaceful picnic by the water's edge.

The Tapantí National Park, located on the eastern edge of the Orosi Valley, is another natural attraction that draws visitors to the area. This park, part of the larger La Amistad International Park, is one of the most biodiverse areas in Costa Rica and is home to a wide variety of plant and animal species. The park's dense cloud forests, waterfalls, and rivers create a lush and vibrant environment that is a haven for wildlife. Visitors to Tapantí can explore the park's trails, which range from easy walks to more challenging hikes, and experience the beauty and tranquility of one of Costa Rica's lesser-known national parks.

The Orosi Valley is also a place where visitors can experience the warmth and hospitality of the local communities. The valley's residents are proud of their cultural heritage and are eager to share their traditions, stories, and way of life with visitors. Many of the valley's small towns and villages have retained their traditional character, with narrow streets, colorful houses, and vibrant markets where locals sell fresh produce, handmade crafts, and other goods. Visitors who take the time to explore these communities will find a welcoming atmosphere and a strong sense of community that is often lacking in more touristy areas.

In terms of accommodations, the Orosi Valley offers a range of options that cater to different tastes and budgets. Visitors can choose from rustic lodges, cozy bed-and-breakfasts, or more upscale boutique hotels, many of which are set in scenic locations that offer stunning views of the valley and surrounding mountains. Staying in one of these accommodations allows visitors to fully immerse themselves in the tranquility and natural beauty of the Orosi Valley while enjoying the comforts of a well-appointed retreat.

The culinary traditions of the Orosi Valley are another aspect of the region that should not be overlooked. The valley's fertile land produces an abundance of fresh fruits, vegetables, and other ingredients that are used to create delicious and wholesome meals. Local restaurants and cafes often serve traditional Costa Rican dishes, such as gallo pinto (a rice and bean dish), casado (a plate with rice, beans, meat, and salad), and tamales (corn dough filled with meat or vegetables and wrapped in banana leaves). Visitors can also enjoy fresh coffee, baked goods, and other treats made from locally sourced ingredients, providing a taste of the region's culinary heritage.

For those interested in learning more about the history and culture of the Orosi Valley, there are several cultural events and festivals held throughout the year. These events often feature traditional music, dance, and other cultural expressions that highlight the region's rich heritage. Participating in these events offers visitors a deeper understanding of the valley's cultural identity and the importance of preserving its traditions for future generations.

In conclusion, the Orosi Valley is a hidden gem in Costa Rica that offers a unique and enriching experience for tourists seeking to explore the country's coffee heartland. With its rich history, stunning landscapes, and warm local communities, the valley provides a journey into the heart of Costa Rican culture and tradition. Whether you are exploring the coffee plantations, hiking through the lush forests, or simply enjoying the peaceful atmosphere of the valley, a visit to the Orosi Valley offers a chance to connect with the natural and cultural heritage of Costa Rica in a way that is both authentic and memorable. For those who seek to discover the hidden treasures of this beautiful country, the Orosi Valley is a destination that should not be missed.

Santa Teresa

Located on the Nicoya Peninsula of Costa Rica, Santa Teresa is a tiny, charming beach town that has gradually been known as one of the best places in the nation for yoga and surfing retreats. Santa Teresa, tucked away from the busy tourist areas, provides a special fusion of unspoiled beauty, relaxed charm, and a thriving local and visitor population that is attracted to the area's immaculate beaches, top-notch surf, and peaceful setting. Santa Teresa offers the perfect environment for travelers looking for a place that blends adventure and leisure. Here, they may lose themselves in the rhythm of the waves, the tranquility of yoga, and the basic joys of living in a tropical paradise.

The gorgeous beaches that run for kilometers along the Pacific coast, with their silky white sand, swaying palm trees, and breathtaking sunsets, are the first thing that make Santa Teresa so alluring. Playa Santa Teresa, the town's principal beach, is considered by many to be among the most beautiful in Costa Rica. Its golden sands and pristine seas make it the ideal setting for a range of activities. The beach is a paradise for those who want to relax, whether it's by sunbathing, taking long walks along the water's edge, or just listening to the sound of the waves. This is due to its natural beauty and comparatively empty shoreline.

But what has really made Santa Teresa famous is the surf. A rising international surfing community has been drawn to the area by its reliable waves, which are appropriate for surfers of all skill levels. Depending on the season and tide, Santa Teresa's surf breakers are renowned for their quality, providing both strong and soft waves. Because of its southwesterly position, the beach consistently receives waves from several directions, making it a dependable place to surf all year round.

There are many surf schools and instructors in Santa Teresa that provide courses for novices of all ability levels. The fundamentals of paddling, standing up, and riding waves in white water are usually covered in these classes, which then progressively go on to more complex methods as pupils develop confidence. Learning to surf at Santa Teresa is a pleasant experience because of the warm water, welcoming environment, and encouraging instructors. Many novices fall in love with surfing right away.

Santa Teresa's beaches provide a range of breakers that suit various tastes and styles for surfers with greater expertise. Just south of Santa Teresa, Playa Carmen is a well-liked location for intermediate surfers because of its long, gentle waves, which are ideal for honing skills and performing tricks. A little farther north, Playa Hermosa is a popular among experienced surfers seeking a challenge because of its stronger waves and smaller lineup. Surfers can find the ideal wave to fit their skills and tastes thanks to the variety of surf places in and around Santa Teresa.

Along with its surf culture, Santa Teresa has grown to be a popular destination for yoga practitioners, who are attracted to the town's peaceful surroundings and all-encompassing way of life. Santa Teresa has seen a boom in yoga and health retreats, giving guests the opportunity to hone their skills in an environment that encourages rest, awareness, and a connection to the natural world. A tranquil and immersive experience is offered by the eco-friendly hotels and spa facilities that host many of these retreats, which are tucked away in the verdant forest.

Santa Teresa offers yoga sessions at a number of venues, including private studios surrounded by tropical greenery and beachfront shalas with views of the ocean. From novices to expert yogis, these programs accommodate all skill levels and often include aspects of the surrounding landscape, such meditating under the rainforest canopy or practicing to the sound of the waves. Yoga and Santa Teresa's natural beauty combine to provide a potent experience that revitalizes the body and the mind.

Santa Teresa provides a variety of retreats that integrate daily yoga practice with other wellness practices including meditation, breathwork, and healthy nutrition for those looking for a more intense yoga experience. These retreats provide a comprehensive approach to wellbeing by often include sessions on subjects like personal development, nutrition, and mindfulness. These retreats provide participants the chance to meet like-minded people, experiment with new techniques, and develop a better knowledge of who they are and how they relate to the world.

In addition to yoga and surfing, Santa Teresa has a plethora of additional activities that let tourists experience the region's natural beauty and cultural diversity. The beautiful forest that envelops the town is home to a wide range of species, such as sloths, howler monkeys, and vibrant birds. Through the forest, hiking routes lead to magnificent vistas with expansive views of the coastline, secret waterfalls, and natural ponds. Investigating these pathways offers an opportunity to feel the peace and quiet of the forest while also establishing a connection with the local flora and animals.

A trip to the neighboring Cabo Blanco Nature Reserve, Costa Rica's first national park, is one of the most well-liked activities in Santa Teresa. The reserve, which was created in 1963 and is a conservation model, provides a beautiful setting where guests may stroll through thick woodland, see animals, and relax on remote beaches. Numerous bird species, coatis, and white-faced capuchin monkeys are among the many animals that call the reserve home. Visitors of all fitness levels may enjoy Cabo Blanco's paths, which vary from leisurely strolls to strenuous excursions.

Santa Teresa's attraction as a wellness resort is increased by its position on the Nicoya Peninsula, one of the world's five Blue Zones. Centenarians are common in the Nicoya Peninsula, which is renowned as a "blue zone" where people live longer, healthier lives. Santa Teresa residents' long lifespans are a result of their lifestyle, which is defined by a balanced diet, frequent exercise, close social ties, and a close connection with the natural world. By savoring the fresh, locally produced food, taking part in neighborhood activities, or just accepting the slower pace of life, visitors to Santa Teresa may get a personal look at this way of life.

Another feature of Santa Teresa is its gastronomic scene, which offers a wide variety of eating alternatives to suit a range of palates. Local vegetables, seafood, and healthy eating are highlighted on the menus of many Santa Teresa restaurants, which concentrate on using fresh, organic foods. The cuisine of Santa Teresa reflects the town's cosmopolitan vibe, ranging from foreign cuisine like sushi and Italian pasta to traditional Costa Rican meals like gallo pinto and ceviche. The focus on farm-to-table methods and sustainability guarantees that the food is not only tasty but also consistent with community ideals.

The town's nightlife, which consists of a variety of beach

bars, live music venues, and casual get-togethers, reflects its laid-back atmosphere. There are many of chances to have a drink, take in some music, and mingle with residents and other tourists, even if Santa Teresa isn't as well-known for its nightlife as other of Costa Rica's bigger towns. Visitors may enjoy a drink or a refreshing beer while watching the sun set at the beach bars in Santa Teresa, which often throw sunset parties. The town's nightlife often features live music, ranging from acoustic to reggae acts, which enhances the feeling of connection and community.

Santa Teresa has a variety of lodging options, from luxurious beachfront homes to affordable hostels, so guests may choose a place to stay that meets their requirements and tastes. With eco-friendly features like solar energy, water conservation, and the use of natural materials, many of Santa Teresa's lodging options are made with sustainability in mind. By staying in one of these lodgings, guests may take use of contemporary conveniences while reducing their environmental effect.

A hidden treasure for those looking for a more unique Costa Rican experience, Santa Teresa has maintained its charm and authenticity despite its increasing popularity. The town's dedication to protecting its natural surroundings, helping out small companies, and encouraging a feeling of community makes sure that it will always be a unique destination for both tourists and locals. Santa Teresa provides a unique and satisfying experience that lingers long after you go, whether you come for the surf, the yoga, or just to unwind and take in the beauty of the surroundings.

A hidden treasure in Costa Rica, Santa Teresa provides the ideal fusion of yoga, surfing, and scenic beauty. It is the perfect place for anyone looking for adventure and leisure because of its immaculate beaches, reliable waves, and serene surroundings. Santa Teresa is a must-visit location for anybody wishing to discover Costa Rica's hidden gems because of its thriving community, rich culture, and dedication to sustainability. Santa Teresa welcomes you to experience its charm and adopt the pura vida way of life that characterizes this unique region of the globe, regardless of your level of experience surfing, your devotion to yoga, or your appreciation of the warmth of the local way of life and the beauty of nature.

Barra Honda

For those who are keen to discover Costa Rica's lesser-known treasures, Barra Honda, a hidden jewel in the northwest province of Guanacaste, provides an intriguing and one-of-a-kind experience. Barra Honda transports tourists far below the surface of the Earth, into a realm of subterranean wonders that few get to see, in contrast to many of Costa Rica's attractions, which are often above ground and illuminated by sunshine. Best renowned for its vast network of limestone caverns, this national park offers a fascinating fusion of adventure, natural beauty, and geological importance, making it a must-visit location for anybody wishing to see Costa Rica from a new angle.

Despite being a very tiny park—about 2,295 hectares—Barra Honda National Park is home to one of Central America's most remarkable cave systems. The caverns in the park were created millions of years ago, during the Miocene Epoch, when the sea covered a large portion of the region. These ancient coral reefs and marine sediments were exposed to the elements as they were pushed to the surface by the slow raising of the land and the movement of tectonic plates. The complex system of caves and passageways that we see today was formed when rainwater that was somewhat acidic from dissolved carbon dioxide crept into the earth and gradually dissolved the limestone.

Not only are these caverns there, but the variety and intricacy of the formations they contain are what really set Barra Honda apart. Although there are over 40 caverns in the park, only a small number are open to the public because of safety concerns and the fragile nature of the cave ecosystems. Nonetheless, the accessible caverns provide a window into a hidden realm that is both enigmatic and exquisite. The breathtaking collection of stalactites, stalagmites, columns, and flowstones seen within these caverns was created over thousands of years by the gradual trickle of mineral-rich water.

Hiking through the park's dry tropical forest, which is home to a diversity of plant and animal species, is the first step in exploring Barra Honda's caverns. Deciduous trees that shed their leaves during the dry months define the forest, which has a unique dry season. As a result, the scenery varies significantly with the seasons. The forest seems more parched during the dry season, with barren trees and a mat of fallen leaves, but during the rainy season it is lush and verdant. Barra Honda is a fascinating location for caving aficionados as well as anyone curious in Costa Rica's distinctive ecosystems because of its variety of habitats.

Monkeys, deer, armadillos, and other bird species are among the park's animals that visitors may come upon while exploring the woodland. From the howler monkeys' cries to the rustle of leaves under your feet, the forest's noises create an engrossing experience that prepares you for the adventure ahead. The reward that awaits you underneath makes the relatively difficult journey to the caves—which includes some steep parts—well worth the effort.

Although it is doubtful that tourists would come across the deadly fer-de-lance snake, known locally as terciopelo, within the cave, Terciopelo Cave is the most visited cave in Barra Honda. The easiest to reach among the park's caverns, Terciopelo Cave is often the first place tourists go. Visitors must descend a vertical ladder that descends about 17 meters (56 feet) into the cavern in order to access the cave. Those who are not used to caving may find this descent a little frightening, but every trip is accompanied by knowledgeable experts who make it safe.

Visitors are welcomed with a captivating display of rock formations as soon as they enter Terciopelo Cave. Delicate stalactites, which dangle like icicles from above, decorate the cave's walls and ceilings, while stalagmites, which rise like old pillars, are scattered throughout the floor. These structures have sometimes grown together to create columns that are quite tall. The structures' patterns and shapes vary greatly; some have more abstract features, while others resemble drapery. The gentle illumination of headlamps illuminates the cave's natural characteristics, bringing out the fine textures of the rock and creating spooky shadows.

The sensation of calm and quiet that permeates Terciopelo Cave is among its most outstanding features. The only noises in the cave are the gentle echo of footsteps and the occasional trickle of water. The air is cold and humid. Visitors may fully enjoy the cave's historic beauty and reflect on the vast amount of time that these formations have evolved over thanks to its calm. Being within Terciopelo Cave is an awe-inspiring and humbling experience that provides a unique chance to get up close and personal with a portion of nature that is often out of sight.

Barra Honda National Park provides access to many caverns, each with distinctive characteristics, in addition to Terciopelo Cave. The Santa Ana Cave is one such cave, renowned for its peculiar formations and tight passageways. Compared to Terciopelo Cave, Santa Ana Cave receives fewer visitors, but for those who are ready to brave its more constrained areas, it provides a more daring experience. Flowstones that resemble frozen waterfalls and other formations that are almost sculptural in their intricacy may be seen within Santa Ana

Cave. The cave is a popular among more seasoned cavers because of its winding passageways and chambers, which foster a spirit of exploration and discovery.

Nicoa Cave, which has a noteworthy archeological past, is another noteworthy cave in the park. The indigenous Chorotega people utilized Nicoa Cave as a burial place in the past, and excavations have revealed tools, ceramics, and human remains that provide light on the area's pre-Columbian past. The cave's historical importance makes it a significant location for anybody interested in Costa Rica's cultural legacy, even if it is not as physically impressive as some of the other caves in the park.

The caverns of Barra Honda are significant ecologically in addition to their geological and archeological importance. Numerous species that are uniquely suited to the chilly, dark environment may be found in the caverns. Among them are insects, spiders, and bats, some of which are unique to Costa Rica. The administration of the park takes care to safeguard these sensitive ecosystems, making sure that human activity doesn't upset the delicate balance of life in the caverns. To help protect the caverns for future generations, visitors must abide by stringent rules, such as sticking on specified trails and not touching the formations.

Barra Honda National Park has other things for tourists to explore outside of the caverns. Hiking routes in the park lead to picturesque vantage spots with expansive views of the Gulf of Nicoya and the Tempisque River Valley. These vantage points are excellent for photography and birding since, on clear days, one can see all the way to the Pacific Ocean. A diverse range of species, such as orchids, bromeliads, and other tropical plants that flourish in the dry forest habitat, may also be found in the park.

Barra Honda includes a modest visitor center that offers information on the caverns, the surrounding flora and wildlife, and the indigenous history of the area for visitors who are interested in learning more about the park's natural and cultural past. Visitors may better understand the significance of the park and its preservation efforts thanks to the center's displays, which also highlight how crucial it is to preserve these rare natural treasures.

Part of what makes Barra Honda National Park so unique is that it is not as well-known as some of Costa Rica's other national parks. Due to the park's relative obscurity, it is often less crowded, giving visitors a more private and tranquil view of the caverns and the surrounding forest. One of the primary attractions for those who choose to explore Barra Honda outside the usual route is the feeling of isolation and closeness to nature.

Because Barra Honda is situated in a rather distant region and lacks the infrastructure of other well-known tourist spots, visiting the park needs some preparation. But for those that want to travel, this is also what makes the trip fulfilling. The administration of the park offers guided tours of the caverns, and the park is accessible by road from the town of Nicoya. These trips are conducted by experienced guides who have received caving training and are acquainted with the environment and history of the area. These guides' presence guarantees that guests may securely explore the caverns and discover the area's cultural and environmental value.

For those interested in discovering Costa Rica's subterranean wonders, Barra Honda is a hidden jewel that provides an absolutely unique experience. While the park's historical sites give insights into the life of the indigenous people who formerly lived the area, its vast cave system, which was developed over millions of years, offers an intriguing look into the region's geological past. Barra Honda is a place that is both informative and breathtaking because of the beauty and peace of the caverns as well as the abundant biodiversity of the nearby forest. Barra Honda is a must-visit location for anybody looking to discover Costa Rica's hidden gems.

CHAPTER 6

ADVENTURES AND ACTIVITIES

Thrilling Activities for Solo Travellers

With a wide range of exhilarating activities to suit both thrill-seekers and those who just want to take in the breathtaking natural scenery, Costa Rica is a haven for adventure-seeking single travelers. This Central American gem offers a plethora of opportunities for solo travelers to experience Costa Rica's wonders on their own terms, whether they are seeking to push their limits through extreme sports, immerse themselves in the wild beauty of rainforests and volcanoes, or connect with the rich biodiversity for which the country is known.

Zip-lining across Costa Rica's gorgeous jungle canopy is one of the most thrilling experiences for lone travelers. Costa Rica is well known for its zip-line experiences, which give you a bird's-eye perspective of the rainforest below as you swing far above the trees. Flying through the air while taking in the sights and sounds of the forest is an exhilarating and breathtaking experience. Zip-line trips are especially popular in the Arenal region, which is home to the well-known Arenal Volcano. These experiences often include many platforms and lines of various lengths and speeds. You will get the opportunity to see animals including sloths, birds, and monkeys as you soar over the skies, making this an experience that will never be forgotten.

White-water rafting is another must-try sport in Costa Rica for thrill-seekers who would rather be closer to the ground. With mild to difficult rapids, the nation's rivers—fed by precipitation from the highlands and volcanoes—offer ideal rafting conditions. One of the world's top white-water rafting locations, the Pacuare River provides an exhilarating journey through pristine rainforest, complete with heart-pounding rapids and serene sections where you can appreciate the natural beauty of the area. It is simple for lone travelers to sign up for guided rafting trips, which include all the gear and safety instructions you need to enjoy the experience worry-free.

Surfers of all skill levels love Costa Rica's coastline because of its warm seas and reliable waves. Surfing gives lone travelers an opportunity to get in touch with the water and try their talents in some of the top surf locations on the planet. The Nicoya Peninsula is well-known for its surf culture and has waves that are appropriate for both novice and expert surfers, especially on the beaches of Santa Teresa, Nosara, and Tamarindo. There are several surf schools and instructors who can teach you the fundamentals and have you surfing quickly if you're new to the sport. Even the most experienced surfers will find the strong waves and reef breaks at Playa Hermosa and Pavones to be a challenge for those with more expertise. For single tourists, surfing in Costa Rica is a fulfilling experience because of the friendly surfers and the relaxed vibe of the coastal communities.

Another exciting activity you shouldn't miss is exploring Costa Rica's volcanoes. Numerous active and inactive volcanoes may be found across the nation, each of which offers distinctive scenery and exciting adventure options. One of Costa Rica's most famous volcanoes, the Arenal Volcano, is encircled by a national park with a range of activities for lone tourists. You may discover the volcanic environment, complete with lava fields, hot springs, and a lush jungle, by hiking the paths around Arenal. Hiking through deep forest to reach the breathtaking 70-meter La Fortuna Waterfall, which is close to the volcano's base, is a worthwhile experience that culminates with the opportunity to cool down in the cold pool at the foot of the falls. For a more strenuous experience, think about trekking to the top of Cerro Chato, an extinct volcano close to Arenal. There, you'll be rewarded with sweeping views of the surroundings and a crater lake.

Another kind of volcanic experience may be found at the Rincon de la Vieja Volcano in the Guanacaste area. Part of a broader national park, this active volcano is well-known for its geothermal activity, which includes fumaroles, boiling mud pots, and natural hot springs. The park's varied habitats, which include cloud forest and dry woodland, provide a distinctive setting for exploration and trekking. The park's pathways, which wind through a range of landscapes and provide opportunities to witness animals including coatis, howler monkeys, and colorful birds, are peaceful for lone visitors. Though it's a strenuous walk, the views of the surrounding countryside and the Pacific Ocean from the top of Rincon de la Vieja make the effort worthwhile.

Diving and snorkeling in Costa Rica's coastal waters provide an opportunity to see the lively underwater world for those who are captivated by the ocean and marine life. Some of the nation's top diving locations may be found along the Pacific coast, especially in the vicinity of the Osa Peninsula and the Golfo Dulce. Off the Osa Peninsula, Cano Island is a marine reserve renowned for its pristine seas and plethora of marine life. If you dive here, you may observe schools of fish, sea turtles, rays, sharks, and even gorgeous coral reefs for yourself. Because the shallow seas around Cano Island provide good visibility and the opportunity to get up close and personal with a variety of marine life, snorkeling is also quite popular there.

With its warm, clear seas and colorful coral reefs, Costa Rica's Caribbean coast provides great diving and snorkeling conditions. Situated close to Puerto Viejo, the Gandoca-Manzanillo National Wildlife Refuge is a protected region that encompasses both terrestrial and marine habitats. There is an abundance of life on these coral reefs, including angelfish, parrotfish, and many other reef species. This region is accessible to solo travelers of all ability levels since snorkeling lets you enjoy the splendor of the coral reefs without the need for diving gear.

Sea kayaking is a great method to see Costa Rica's coastline and rivers for lone visitors who would rather remain on land but still want to feel the excitement of the ocean. The Nicoya Peninsula is a great place to go sea kayaking because of its serene coves and mangrove estuaries. You may witness a multitude of animals when paddling through the mangroves, such as crocodiles, monkeys, and other bird species. While the open ocean is a more difficult experience for those wishing to test their paddling prowess, the serene waters of the mangroves provide a serene environment for exploration. For lone travelers, kayak trips are offered, complete with all the gear and instruction needed to guarantee a fun and safe trip.

Canyoning, also referred to as canyoneering, is another exhilarating sport for lone travelers in Costa Rica. This adventure sport combines swimming, climbing, and rappelling to go through tight valleys and drop waterfalls. Canyoning is ideal in Costa Rica's untamed jungles, which include precipitous cliffs and thundering waterfalls. The Arenal region is a well-liked location for this activity because to its many waterfalls and steep gorges. A heart-pounding adventure that blends the thrill of rappelling with the splendor of the surrounding environment, guided canyoning trips lead you through some of the most picturesque and difficult canyons in the area.

There are plenty of chances for lone hikers and trekkers to see Costa Rica's varied ecosystems on foot. Numerous routes wind across the nation's national parks and reserves, passing through a range of environments from cloud forests and rainforests to coastal plains and volcanic craters. One of the most well-known hiking locations in Costa Rica is the Monteverde Cloud Forest Reserve, which is situated in the central highlands. A wide variety of plant and animal species, including the elusive dazzling quetzal, one of the most exquisite birds in the world, may be found in the reserve's foggy cloud woods. Experience the enchantment of the cloud forest, with its tall trees, dangling vines, and colorful epiphytes, by hiking Monteverde's pathways.

Situated on the isolated Osa Peninsula, Corcovado National Park is another great place to go trekking. One of the world's most biodiverse locations, Corcovado provides some of Costa Rica's most difficult but rewarding walks due to its untamed landscape. You may witness a variety of species, such as jaguars, tapirs, and scarlet macaws, on the park's paths, which wind through primary rainforest, along immaculate beaches, and over rivers. A popular option for daring lone travelers, the multi-day hike from the park's entrance to the Sirena Ranger Station offers an immersive experience in one of Costa Rica's most untamed and isolated regions.

Many of Costa Rica's adventure activities are made to be sustainable and eco-friendly because of the country's dedication to conservation and ecotourism. You can be sure that your experience is helping to preserve Costa Rica's natural beauty, whether you're diving in the ocean, rafting down a river, or zip-lining through the jungle. Because of the nation's emphasis on environmentally friendly travel, lone tourists may take part in these activities knowing that they are assisting local communities and preserving the environment.

There are many exciting activities available in Costa Rica for lone tourists, each offering a different approach to see the rich biodiversity and varied landscapes of the nation. Every adventurous tourist may find something to enjoy in Costa Rica, from the exhilarating activities of zip-lining and surfing to the tranquil beauty of trekking through cloud forests and snorkeling on coral reefs. The nation is the perfect place for lone travelers who want to feel the rush of adventure while getting in touch with nature because of its friendly people, dedication to sustainability, and plenty of natural attractions. Costa Rica welcomes you to explore its delights and make lifelong memories, whether your goal is to push yourself via extreme sports or just to take in the splendor of the jungle.

Romantic Escapes for Couples

With a variety of charming locations that appeal to all kinds of tourists, Costa Rica is a haven for couples looking for romantic getaways. This varied and stunning nation offers the ideal setting for romantic adventures that will last a lifetime, whether you're searching for remote beaches, verdant jungles, or opulent lodging. Costa Rica's stunning natural surroundings and friendly locals set the backdrop for a trip full of private moments, stunning landscapes, and shared experiences as soon as you arrive.

The Arenal area, which is home to the well-known Arenal Volcano and the hot springs nearby, is one of the most romantic places in Costa Rica for couples. The breathtaking scenery of the Arenal region is well known, with the volcano's towering shape rising over the verdant jungle to create a dramatic and beautiful scene. A leisurely stroll through Arenal Volcano National Park, where well-kept paths wind past historic lava flows and through lush woods, is a great way for couples to start the day. Immersion in nature is enhanced by the park's varied flora and wildlife, which includes vibrant birds, monkeys, and tropical plants. You'll have many chances to stop and enjoy the expansive views of the volcano and the surrounding countryside as you hike the paths together, making lifelong memories.

Nothing is more soothing than taking a dip in one of the many natural hot springs in the Arenal region after a day of touring. Couples may enjoy a tranquil and romantic experience in these geothermal pools, which are heated by the volcanic activity under the ground. Surrounded by rich flora and often filled with the sounds of the forest, the warm waters provide the ideal environment for rest and renewal. Numerous hot spring resorts in the region provide couples with quiet places to spend time together, including private pools. The peaceful setting and the warm, mineral-rich water combine to produce a sensation of connection and well-being that is perfect for a romantic getaway.

For beach lovers, couples looking for sun, sand, and sea should go to the Nicoya Peninsula on Costa Rica's Pacific coast. Some of the most stunning and remote beaches in the nation may be found on the peninsula, where soft, white sand meets turquoise seas and palm palms swing softly in the wind. The village of Santa Teresa, renowned for its relaxed atmosphere and breathtaking sunsets, is one of the peninsula's most romantic locations. Santa Teresa's broad sections of beach are ideal for romantic strolls, and the sound of the waves provide a calming background to your stroll. You may choose a peaceful place on the beach to see the sun setting and the sky becoming orange, pink, and purple as the day comes to an end. It is difficult to find a more romantic moment than the splendor of the sunset and the tranquility of the beach.

The Nicoya Peninsula provides many of chances for adventure for couples seeking a more active beach experience. The region is renowned for its top-notch surfing, and going surfing with someone may be an enjoyable and uplifting experience. Beginners will love Playa Hermosa or Playa Carmen's mild waves, while surfers with more expertise may test their mettle on Playa Santa Teresa's bigger waves. Following a day of swimming, you may relax at one of the numerous eateries or cafés along the shore, where you can savor delicious seafood and tropical drinks while taking in the waves.

The Osa Peninsula, a secluded and unspoiled region ideal for couples seeking to get away from the throng and spend time in nature, is another romantic location in Costa Rica. One of the planet's most biodiverse locations, Corcovado National Park, is located on the Osa Peninsula. Together, exploring the park provides an opportunity to develop a deep connection with both the natural environment and one another. The park's paths provide many chances for exploration and adventure as they wind past waterfalls, through lush jungle, and along empty beaches. You'll probably come across a range of animals on your journey around the park, such as sloths, monkeys, and colorful birds. Sharing these experiences with your significant other in such an uncontrolled and untamed setting is a really unique experience that fosters a strong feeling of bonding.

Consider booking a room at one of the eco-lodges on the Osa Peninsula for a really exceptional romantic encounter. These lodges often have breathtaking views of the ocean and are situated in isolated locations with rainforests all around. It is simple to forget about the outside world and concentrate on one another because of the emphasis on sustainability and a connection to nature, which heightens the feeling of closeness and solitude. Numerous hotels give guided excursions, such boat rides to explore the mangroves or nighttime walks to see the nocturnal creatures, which provide chances to make enduring memories with one another.

The Papagayo Peninsula on Costa Rica's northern Pacific coast is a great option if you want to combine adventure with leisure. Some of the most opulent resorts in the nation, with top-notch facilities and stunning ocean views, can be found on the peninsula. You may enjoy the best of both worlds when you stay at one of these resorts: the thrill of exploring the surroundings and the relaxation of coming home to an opulent haven at the end of the day. The Papagayo Peninsula is renowned for its immaculate beaches, where you may swim in the glistening seas or just relax in the sun. Together, kayaking and stand-up paddleboarding may be an enjoyable way to explore the coastline, and the quiet bays are perfect for these activities.

For adventurous couples, the Papagayo Peninsula provides a variety of activities in addition to its stunning beaches. A zip-lining adventure through the rainforest, where you can fly above the trees and enjoy breathtaking vistas of the jungle and ocean, is one of the highlights. This is an unforgettable experience that is ideal for sharing with your significant other because of the exhilaration of soaring through the air and the surrounding natural beauty. Following an adventurous day, you may relax with a couples massage at one of the upscale spas on the peninsula, where you can take advantage of treatments that use traditional methods and local ingredients. The ideal approach to round off a day of exploring is to combine rest and renewal.

A trip to the Monteverde Cloud Forest Reserve is essential for couples who have a strong interest in wildlife and environmental preservation. The cloud forest provides an enchanted backdrop for a romantic getaway because of its mist-covered trees and abundant wildlife. The paths in the reserve lead you through a diversity of environments, from open clearings to deep forests, where you may see a variety of plant and animal species. The cloud forest is the perfect spot for a peaceful stroll with your significant other because of its enigmatic and magical atmosphere, which is created by its cold, foggy temperature. Many tourists' top attractions are the opportunity to witness the elusive resplendent quetzal, with its vivid red and green plumage; seeing this with a significant other heightens the sensation of awe.

Numerous eco-lodges that provide comfortable and romantic lodging in the center of the cloud forest may also be found in Monteverde. When you stay at one of these lodges, you may enjoy the beauty of the surrounds from the comfort of your bed while waking up to the sounds of the forest. Numerous resorts provide night walks to see the nocturnal species and guided tours of the area. Monteverde is the perfect place for couples who want to enjoy a romantic getaway while taking in Costa Rica's natural splendor since it offers both comfort and excitement.

The town of Cartago provides a distinctive and romantic getaway for couples who want to see historical and cultural landmarks. One of Costa Rica's oldest cities, Cartago is situated in the Central Valley and is renowned for its rich history and colonial architecture. A highlight of every journey to Cartago is a visit to the Basilica of Nuestra Señora de los Ángeles, one of the most significant places of worship in Costa Rica. The basilica is a lovely location for a group exploration because of its magnificent architecture and calm ambiance. Following your visit to the basilica, you may stroll around the town's streets, taking in the colonial architecture and pausing for a cup of Costa Rican coffee at a neighborhood café.

Another romantic location for couples is the Orosi Valley, which is located just outside of Cartago. The valley is renowned for its gorgeous scenery, which includes quaint towns, coffee plantations, and undulating hills. The Orosi Valley is a great destination for a leisurely drive, where you may pause to take in the breathtaking scenery and visit the little communities. One of the oldest churches in Costa Rica, the colonial church of San José de Orosi, is a must-see. The chapel is a great place for introspection because of its serene surroundings and elegant but basic style. There are also a number of hot springs in the Orosi Valley where you may unwind and bathe in the warm, mineral-rich waters while taking in the scenery.

The Caribbean coast's Puerto Viejo district provides a charming and distinctive getaway for couples seeking a less-traveled experience. Puerto Viejo is well-known for its beautiful beaches, lively culture, and relaxed atmosphere. The local food, music, and architecture all reflect the town's Afro-Caribbean origins, which combine to create a vibrant and rich ambiance ideal for a romantic retreat. You may swim in the warm waves, sunbathe on the fine sand, or explore the neighboring coral reefs at Puerto Viejo's beaches, such Playa Cocles and Punta Uva, which provide the ideal environment for a day of leisure.

For couples that like being outside, Puerto Viejo is an excellent vacation. Snorkeling at the neighboring Cahuita National Park is a great way to explore the coral reefs and view a range of marine life, including as rays, sea turtles, and colorful fish. Along the park's pathways, you may also explore the coastal rainforest, which is home to a variety of bird species, sloths, and monkeys. You may return to Puerto Viejo after an adventurous day and have a romantic evening at one of the numerous restaurants in the area, where you can enjoy the tastes of Caribbean food while listening to reggae music.

There are many romantic getaway options in Costa Rica for couples, and each one provides a unique and memorable experience. Costa Rica offers the ideal backdrop for a romantic vacation, whether you're exploring the beautiful jungles of Arenal, relaxing on the immaculate beaches of the Nicoya Peninsula, or taking in the local culture of Puerto Viejo. The nation is the perfect place for couples wishing to build enduring memories together because of its varied attractions, friendly people, and stunning natural surroundings. Costa Rica welcomes you to explore its treasures and take in the romance of this stunning nation, regardless of your preference for adventure, leisure, or a mix of the two.

Family Fun

Families seeking adventure, excitement, and meaningful activities that appeal to all ages will find Costa Rica to be the perfect place. Everyone, from young children to grandparents, may find something to enjoy and participate in during family holidays in this nation because of its rich natural beauty, varied ecosystems, and friendly culture. Costa Rica provides a variety of activities that suit all interests and ages, whether your family wants to spend time together in a stunning environment, explore lush jungles, or learn about the marvels of the ocean.

With its breathtaking scenery and plethora of activities, the Arenal Volcano area is one of Costa Rica's most well-liked family vacation spots. The Arenal Volcano, a magnificent and still-active volcano that dominates the surrounding rainforest, is the focal point of this region. With a variety of adventure, leisure, and educational activities that everyone can enjoy, the region around Arenal is ideal for families. Visiting the Arenal Volcano National Park, where you can join guided tours that explain the volcano's geological history as well as the many flora and wildlife that flourish there, is one of the highlights for many families. Families with kids may easily pick a path that works for them since the park's trails range in complexity. You may see howler monkeys, toucans, and other animals while strolling around the park, which will captivate both kids and adults.

Families may unwind and rest in one of the several hot springs in the Arenal region after seeing the park. Families will enjoy the tranquil atmosphere of these naturally occurring geothermal pools, which are heated by the volcano. Numerous hot spring resorts in the region provide family-friendly amenities, such as smaller pools for little children and spaces where parents may unwind with a bath. This is a great place to spend a leisurely day or evening because of the warm water and lovely surroundings.

Manuel Antonio National Park, which is situated on the

Pacific coast of Costa Rica, is another fantastic family vacation spot. With good cause, this park is among the most visited in the nation. It provides a unique blend of immaculate beaches, verdant rainforests, and a wealth of animals, all within a manageably small region that is fun for families to explore. Families will love the park's beaches because of its serene, warm waters, which are great for swimming and sand play. Families may enjoy short treks on the park's jungle paths, which are suitable for hikers of all ages. Children and adults alike will be delighted to witness monkeys, sloths, and vibrant birds as you stroll through the forest.

The chance to go on a guided tour with a naturalist who can identify the many kinds of flora and animals that call Manuel Antonio home is one of the highlights of the trip. In addition to being instructive, these excursions enhance children's park exploration experiences. The entire family may enjoy and learn from seeing animals in their natural environment, learning about the rainforest ecology, and realizing the value of conservation.

Additionally, family may enjoy water sports like kayaking and snorkeling on Manuel Antonio's beaches. Diverse fish and other marine life may be seen on the colorful coral reefs that grow in the park's bays' placid waters. There are also kayaking trips offered, which are an excellent opportunity to see the surrounding islands and shoreline. These kid-friendly activities provide a unique viewpoint on the splendor of Costa Rica's marine habitats.

Families seeking outdoor adventure will have a memorable day in the Monteverde Cloud Forest Reserve. This well-known reserve, which is situated in Costa Rica's central highlands, is renowned for its distinct habitats, abundant wildlife, and misty cloud forests. Families wishing to get away from the heat and humidity of the lowlands will love Monteverde's cool environment and charming ambiance. The reserve's well-kept paths meander through thick woodland, showcasing a remarkable array of flora and fauna, such as orchids, bromeliads, monkeys, and the elusive resplendent quetzal, one of the world's most exquisite birds.

The canopy tour, which allows you to explore the treetops on a number of suspended bridges and zip lines, is one of the most thrilling family-friendly activities in Monteverde. A unique view of the cloud forest can be had by crossing the hanging bridges, which give you a close-up look at the canopy and a chance to see the plants and animals that flourish well above the forest floor. With breathtaking views of the forest below, the zip lines offer the more daring a thrilling journey over the trees. These trips provide the ideal balance of fun and instruction, making them appropriate for older kids and teenagers.

Apart from the canopy excursions, Monteverde has other family-friendly attractions including nighttime walks, hummingbird feeders, and butterfly gardens. The butterfly gardens provide a chance to get up close and personal with a range of Costa Rican butterfly species while learning about their life cycles and habits. Numerous vibrant hummingbirds are drawn to the hummingbird feeders, and their swift, scuttling motions are likely to enthrall kids. However, as many creatures are most active after dark, night hikes provide families the chance to explore the cloud forest. A guide can assist you see nocturnal animals like bats, frogs, and insects, which will make your stay much more exciting.

The Caribbean coast of Costa Rica, especially the region around Cahuita and Puerto Viejo, provides a wealth of chances for families who are interested in marine life to explore the underwater environment. Because of the wide variety of marine life found on the coral reefs off the shore, diving and snorkeling are popular pastimes. Cahuita National Park's tranquil waters and readily accessible reefs make it a great place for families. In the shallow seas, even small children may enjoy snorkeling and witness marine life, including sea turtles and colorful fish. Along the park's pathways, you may also explore the coastal rainforest, home to a variety of bird species, sloths, and monkeys.

The Gandoca-Manzanillo Wildlife Refuge, which preserves both terrestrial and marine habitats, is another point of interest along the Caribbean coast. Sea turtles use the refuge's beaches as nesting grounds, and if you go there during the nesting season, you may be able to observe these amazing animals depositing their eggs or watch as young turtles go out to sea. Families have a rare chance to learn about the value of animal protection via this very touching and instructive event.

The Guanacaste area on Costa Rica's northwest Pacific coast is a great place for families looking for a combination of adventure and leisure. This region is well-known for its diverse variety of activities, dry tropical woods, and stunning beaches. With their gentle sand and placid waves, Guanacaste beaches like Playa Conchal and Playa Flamingo are ideal for families. These beaches are perfect for lounging in the sun, swimming, and creating sandcastles. Numerous resorts in this region are family-friendly, with features including kid-friendly clubs, swimming pools, and kid-friendly events.

Guanacaste provides adventure in the surrounding area in addition to its beaches. Families may explore volcanic landscapes, see animals, and engage in outdoor activities like hiking, horseback riding, and river cruises at the region's several national parks, such as Rincon de la Vieja and Palo Verde. Families will especially like Rincon de la Vieja National Park because of its active volcano, bubbling mud pots, and hot springs. All ages may enjoy the park's paths, and getting a close-up look at geothermal activity is an exciting and instructive experience.

Families may go to some of Guanacaste's traditional towns, including Nicoya or Liberia, for a more cultural experience. Along with chances to learn about Costa Rican history and culture, these communities give a window into the local way of life. Families may experience the rich culture of the area by going to local markets, going to a traditional fiesta, or watching a rodeo, to name a few activities.

A trip to Tortuguero National Park on the Caribbean coast of Costa Rica is essential for families that value nature and conservation. One of the most significant sea turtle breeding locations in the Western Hemisphere is Tortuguero, and the park provides a rare chance to see these amazing animals in their own environment. The nesting season, which often lasts from July to October for green sea turtles, is the ideal time to go. Families may see the nesting process via guided excursions, which are often held at night and provide an instructive and breathtaking experience.

Another notable feature of Tortuguero is its system of canals and waterways, which are accessible by kayak or boat. Monkeys, sloths, crocodiles, and a diverse range of bird species are among the many animal species that may be seen on these trips. Families wishing to see Costa Rica's more untamed side will love the park's feeling of adventure created by its secluded position and beautiful surroundings.

Numerous family-friendly activities are available in Costa Rica, offering chances for enjoyment, exploration, and education for people of all ages. Costa Rica is the ideal destination for an unforgettable family holiday, whether you're exploring the Arenal volcanoes, unwinding on the Manuel Antonio beaches, or exploring the animals of Tortuguero. The nation is the perfect place for families wishing to build enduring experiences because of its stunning natural surroundings, abundant biodiversity, and kind people. Costa Rica welcomes you to explore its beauties and feel the thrill of traveling this beautiful country with your loved ones, regardless of your preference for adventure, leisure, or a mix of the two.

Kid-Friendly Attractions

Costa Rica is a treasure trove of kid-friendly attractions that cater to the curiosity and energy of young travelers while providing rich, educational experiences. The country's diverse ecosystems, warm climate, and welcoming culture make it an ideal destination for families with children of all ages. From exploring vibrant rainforests to discovering marine life along the coasts, Costa Rica offers a wide range of activities that engage children's imaginations, satisfy their sense of adventure, and foster a love for the natural world. This detailed guide will take you through some of the best attractions in Costa Rica that are sure to delight and inspire young visitors.

One of the top attractions for kids in Costa Rica is the La Paz Waterfall Gardens, located in the central highlands near the Poás Volcano. This private reserve is a nature lover's paradise and offers a fantastic introduction to Costa Rica's rich biodiversity. The gardens feature a series of stunning waterfalls, which can be easily accessed via well-maintained trails that are suitable for children. The sight of cascading water surrounded by lush vegetation is sure to captivate young minds, and the gentle mist from the falls provides a refreshing break from the tropical heat. Along the trails, kids will have the opportunity to spot colorful birds, butterflies, and other wildlife that inhabit the area.

In addition to the waterfalls, La Paz Waterfall Gardens is home to several animal exhibits that provide a close-up look at some of Costa Rica's most iconic species. The aviary is a highlight, where children can see a variety of tropical birds, including toucans, parrots, and hummingbirds. The butterfly observatory is another must-see, offering a magical experience as kids walk through a large enclosure filled with hundreds of fluttering butterflies. The gardens also feature a serpentarium, a frog exhibit, and a jungle cat exhibit, where children can learn about the different species that call Costa Rica home. The combination of natural beauty and interactive exhibits makes La Paz Waterfall Gardens a perfect day trip for families.

For families interested in marine life, a visit to the Marino Ballena National Park on the Pacific coast is a must. This park, named after the humpback whales that migrate to the area, offers a unique opportunity for children to learn about marine ecosystems and the importance of conservation. One of the park's main attractions is the famous Whale's Tail sandbar, a natural formation that resembles the shape of a whale's tail, which is visible at low tide. Kids will love exploring the sandy beaches, wading in the shallow waters, and searching for seashells and small marine creatures. The gentle waves make it a safe and enjoyable spot for young swimmers.

Whale watching tours are a popular activity in Marino Ballena National Park, especially during the whale migration season, which typically runs from July to October and again from December to March. These tours offer a chance to see humpback whales, dolphins, and other marine life in their natural habitat. The excitement of spotting a whale breaching or a pod of dolphins playing in the waves is an unforgettable experience for children and provides a valuable lesson in the importance of protecting these majestic creatures. Many tour operators in the area are experienced in working with families and make sure that the tours are both educational and engaging for young participants.

Another fantastic kid-friendly attraction in Costa Rica is the Monteverde Cloud Forest Reserve. Located in the central highlands, this reserve is one of the country's most famous natural areas and offers a unique environment that is perfect for exploring with children. The cool, misty climate of the cloud forest provides a refreshing contrast to the warmer coastal areas, and the dense, green canopy creates a sense of wonder and adventure. The reserve's trails are well-marked and suitable for all ages, making it easy for families to explore the different habitats within the forest.

One of the most popular activities in Monteverde is the canopy tour, where families can walk along suspended bridges high above the forest floor. These hanging bridges provide a safe and exciting way for kids to see the forest from a different perspective, offering views of the treetops, waterfalls, and wildlife that live in the canopy. The thrill of walking above the forest, combined with the chance to see birds, monkeys, and other animals up close, makes this an unforgettable experience for children.

In addition to the canopy tours, Monteverde offers a variety of other activities that are perfect for kids. The butterfly garden is a favorite, where children can learn about the life cycle of butterflies and see them up close in a beautifully landscaped enclosure. The hummingbird garden is another highlight, where dozens of hummingbird's zip around, feeding from brightly colored flowers and feeders. For a more immersive experience, families can take a guided night walk, where a naturalist guide will help you spot nocturnal creatures such as frogs, bats, and insects. The chance to explore the forest at night adds an element of adventure that kids are sure to love.

For a more hands-on educational experience, families should consider visiting the Children's Eternal Rainforest, located near Monteverde. This reserve is the largest private reserve in Costa Rica and was established through the efforts of children around the world who raised funds to protect the rainforest. The reserve offers a variety of educational programs and guided tours that are specifically designed for children, teaching them about the importance of conservation and the incredible diversity of life in the rainforest. The trails are easy to navigate and provide opportunities to see a wide range of plants and animals, making it an excellent destination for families who want to combine learning with outdoor fun.

The Tortuguero National Park on the Caribbean coast is another top destination for families with children. Tortuguero is one of the most important nesting sites for sea turtles in the Western Hemisphere, and a visit to the park during the nesting season provides a once-in-a-lifetime experience for young nature lovers. From July to October, families can join guided night tours to watch as female sea turtles come ashore to lay their eggs. Seeing these ancient creatures up close as they perform this remarkable ritual is an awe-inspiring experience that will stay with children for years to come.

In addition to the turtle nesting tours, Tortuguero offers a variety of activities that allow families to explore the park's unique environment. The park's network of canals and waterways can be explored by boat or kayak, providing a chance to see wildlife such as monkeys, sloths, crocodiles, and a rich diversity of bird species. The gentle pace of the boat tours, combined with the opportunity to spot animals in their natural habitat, makes this an enjoyable and educational experience for kids. The park's remote location and lush environment create a sense of adventure that is perfect for families looking to explore the wilder side of Costa Rica.

The Costa Rica Animal Rescue Center, located near San José, is another wonderful destination for families with children. This non-profit organization is dedicated to the rescue, rehabilitation, and release of injured and orphaned wildlife. The center provides a safe haven for animals such as sloths, monkeys, parrots, and anteaters, many of whom have been rescued from illegal pet trade or other harmful situations. A visit to the rescue center offers a unique opportunity for children to learn about the challenges faced by Costa Rica's wildlife and the importance of conservation efforts. The guided tours allow families to see the animals up close and hear their stories, providing a powerful lesson in empathy and the importance of protecting animals.

For a mix of adventure and wildlife, families can visit the Hacienda Barú National Wildlife Refuge on the southern Pacific coast. This private reserve offers a range of activities that are perfect for children, including guided nature walks, zip-lining, and birdwatching tours. The refuge is home to a variety of habitats, including rainforest, mangroves, and beaches, providing plenty of opportunities for exploration. The zip-lining tour is a particular favorite among kids, offering a thrilling ride through the treetops with the chance to see wildlife such as toucans, monkeys, and sloths. The guided nature walks are also a great way to learn about the different ecosystems within the reserve and the species that live there.

Another fun and educational activity for kids in Costa Rica is visiting the Sloth Sanctuary of Costa Rica, located on the Caribbean coast. This sanctuary is dedicated to the rescue, rehabilitation, and research of sloths, and offers tours that allow visitors to learn about these fascinating animals. Children will love seeing the sloths up close and learning about their behavior, diet, and the challenges they face in the wild. The sanctuary's educational programs are designed to be engaging and informative, making it a perfect destination for families who want to learn more about one of Costa Rica's most beloved animals.

The Simón Bolívar Zoo and Botanical Garden in San José is another family-friendly attraction that is sure to delight children. The zoo is home to a variety of native Costa Rican animals, including jaguars, monkeys, and birds, as well as a selection of exotic species from around the world. The botanical garden features a collection of tropical plants and flowers, providing a beautiful setting for a leisurely stroll. The zoo's exhibits are designed to be educational, offering information about the animals and their habitats, as well as the conservation efforts being made to protect them. The zoo's central location makes it a convenient stop for families exploring the capital city.

Finally, no visit to Costa Rica would be complete without spending time on its beautiful beaches. The country's coastline offers a wide range of beaches that are perfect for families with children, with calm waters, soft sand, and plenty of opportunities for swimming, building sandcastles, and exploring tidal pools. Playa Conchal, located on the northern Pacific coast, is one of the most family-friendly beaches in Costa Rica. The beach is known for its crystal-clear waters and soft, white sand made up of tiny crushed shells. The calm waters are perfect for young swimmers, and the nearby coral reefs provide excellent snorkeling opportunities.

Another great beach for families is Playa Manuel Antonio, located within Manuel Antonio National Park. This beach is surrounded by lush rainforest and offers a stunning setting for a day of fun in the sun.

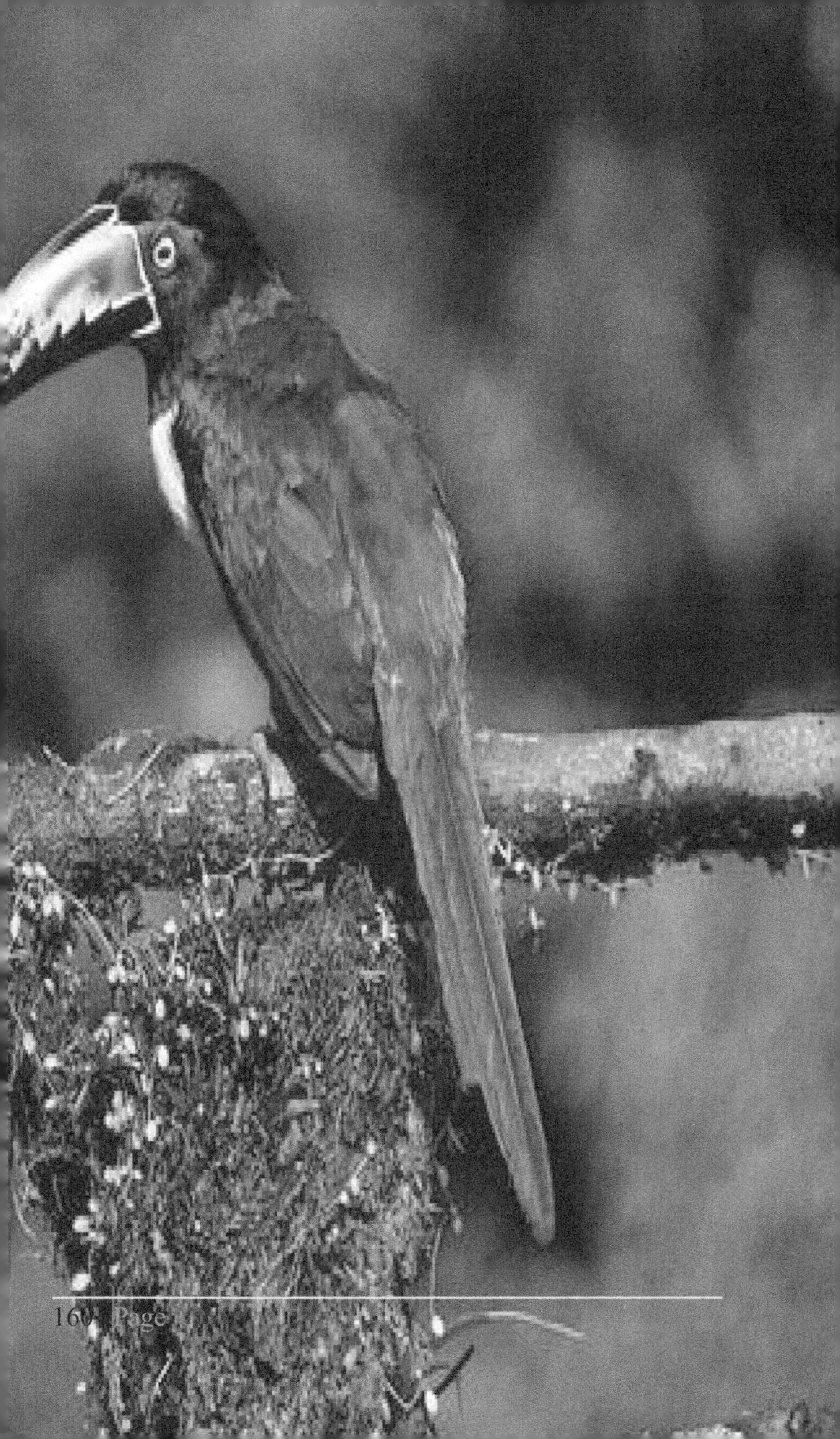

CHAPTER 7

ACCOMMODATION OPTIONS

Luxury Resorts and Boutique Hotels

Costa Rica is a veritable gold mine of kid-friendly sites that provide rich, instructive experiences while satisfying the curiosity and energy of young tourists. Families with kids of all ages find the nation to be the perfect trip because of its varied ecosystems, pleasant temperature, and hospitable culture. Costa Rica provides a variety of activities that stimulate children's imaginations, satiate their sense of adventure, and cultivate a passion for the natural world, from exploring colorful jungles to learning about marine life along the beaches. This comprehensive guide will walk you through some of Costa Rica's top sites, which are guaranteed to inspire and thrill young tourists.

The La Paz Waterfall Gardens, which are situated close to the Poás Volcano in the central highlands, are one of the best places for children to visit Costa Rica. This private reserve provides an excellent introduction to Costa Rica's vast biodiversity and is a nature lover's dream come true. The gardens include a number of beautiful waterfalls that are readily accessible via kid-friendly, well-maintained paths. Young minds will be enthralled by the sight of tumbling water surrounded by rich foliage, and the cool mist from the falls offers a welcome respite from the tropical heat. Children will get the chance to see colorful birds, butterflies, and other local animals along the pathways.

La Paz Waterfall Gardens has a number of animal displays that provide a close-up view of some of Costa Rica's most recognizable animals in addition to the waterfalls. A highlight is the aviary, where kids may see a range of tropical species, such as hummingbirds, parrots, and toucans. Another must-see is the butterfly observatory, where children may have a mystical experience as they pass through a large cage that is home to hundreds of fluttering butterflies. Children may learn about the many animals that inhabit Costa Rica at the gardens' serpentarium, frog display, and jungle cat exhibit. La Paz Waterfall Gardens' interactive displays and scenic surroundings make it the ideal family day trip destination.

A trip to the Pacific coast's Marino Ballena National Park is essential for families with an interest in marine life. Children have a rare chance to learn about marine ecosystems and the value of conservation at this park, which is named for the humpback whales that visit the region. The well-known Whale's Tail sandbar, a naturally occurring structure that resembles a whale's tail and is visible at low tide, is one of the park's primary attractions. Children will enjoy wading in the shallow waters, exploring the sandy beaches, and looking for seashells and other tiny marine life. It's a fun and safe place for little swimmers because of the soft waves.

Particularly during the whale migration season, which

normally lasts from July to October and again from December to March, whale watching trips are a well-liked activity at Marino Ballena National Park. Seeing humpback whales, dolphins, and other marine species in their natural environment is possible with these cruises. Children will never forget the thrill of seeing a whale breach or a group of dolphins playing in the surf, and it teaches them the value of preserving these magnificent animals. Numerous local tour companies have expertise working with families and ensure that the trips are interesting and instructive for young participants.

The Monteverde Cloud Forest Reserve is yet another amazing family-friendly destination in Costa Rica. One of the most well-known natural places in the nation, this reserve is situated in the central highlands and provides a distinctive setting that is ideal for family exploration. A feeling of surprise and adventure is evoked by the cloud forest's deep, green canopy, and its chilly, foggy atmosphere offers a welcome contrast to the warmer coastal regions. Families may easily explore the many ecosystems inside the forest thanks to the reserve's well-marked, kid-friendly routes.

The canopy tour, which allows families to stroll over suspended bridges well above the forest floor, is one of the most well-liked activities in Monteverde. With views of the treetops, waterfalls, and wildlife that inhabits the canopy, these hanging bridges provide children a fun and safe way to see the forest from a new angle. Children will never forget this experience because of the excitement of strolling above the forest and the opportunity to get up close and personal with birds, monkeys, and other creatures.

Apart from the canopy tours, Monteverde has a range of additional kid-friendly activities. A favorite is the butterfly garden, where kids can observe butterflies up close in a beautifully planted area and learn about their life cycle. Another attraction is the hummingbird garden, where hundreds of hummingbirds flutter around, grazing on feeders and vibrant flowers. Families may enjoy a guided night walk for a more engaging experience, during which a naturalist guide will assist you in identifying nocturnal animals including insects, bats, and frogs. Children will adore the opportunity to explore the forest at night since it provides a sense of adventure.

Families looking for a more experiential learning environment may choose to visit the Children's Eternal Rainforest, which is close to Monteverde. Thanks to the efforts of children worldwide who contributed money to save the rainforest, this reserve—which is the biggest private reserve in Costa Rica—was created. Children may learn about the value of conservation and the amazing diversity of life in the rainforest via the reserve's range of kid-friendly educational programs and guided tours. It's a great place for families who want to combine education with outdoor enjoyment since the paths are simple to follow and provide chances to observe a variety of flora and animals.

Another popular spot for families with kids is the Caribbean's

Tortuguero National Park. One of the most significant sea turtle nesting locations in the Western Hemisphere is Tortuguero, and young nature enthusiasts may have a once-in-a-lifetime experience by visiting the park during the nesting season. Families may take part in guided night trips from July to October to see female sea turtles laying their eggs on the beach. Children will remember the breathtaking experience of seeing these ancient animals up close as they carry out this amazing rite for years to come.

Apart from the turtle nesting excursions, Tortuguero provides a range of activities that let families experience the park's distinct surroundings. Boating or kayaking through the park's system of canals and waterways offers the opportunity to see animals including crocodiles, sloths, monkeys, and a wide variety of bird species. For children, this is a fun and instructive experience because of the leisurely boat trips and the chance to see animals in their natural environment. Families wishing to see Costa Rica's more untamed side will love the park's feeling of adventure created by its secluded position and beautiful surroundings.

Another great place for families with kids is the Costa Rica Animal Rescue Center, which is close to San José. Rescue, rehabilitation, and release of wounded and orphaned animals are the main goals of this nonprofit organization. Many of the creatures at the facility, including sloths, monkeys, parrots, and anteaters, have been rescued from dangerous circumstances or the illicit pet trade. Children have a rare chance to learn about the difficulties Costa Rica's wildlife faces and the value of conservation efforts by visiting the rescue facility. Families can view the animals up close and learn about their lives via the guided tours, which provide a potent lesson in empathy and the value of animal protection.

Families may explore the southern Pacific coast's Hacienda Barú National animals Refuge for a combination of animals and adventure. Children may enjoy a variety of kid-friendly activities at this private reserve, such as zip-lining, birding trips, and guided nature hikes. There are many options for exploration since the refuge is home to a range of ecosystems, such as beaches, mangroves, and rainforest. Kids especially love the zip-lining trip, which offers an exhilarating journey over the trees and the opportunity to observe animals like sloths, toucans, and monkeys. Learning about the many ecosystems and animals that inhabit the reserve may also be accomplished via the guided nature walks.

The Sloth Sanctuary of Costa Rica, which is situated on the Caribbean coast, is another entertaining and instructive activity for children in Costa Rica. This sanctuary provides tours for tourists to learn more about these amazing creatures and is devoted to the rescue, rehabilitation, and study of sloths. Youngsters will enjoy getting a close-up look at the sloths and learning about their habits, nutrition, and difficulties in the wild. Families who want to learn more about one of Costa Rica's most cherished creatures will find the refuge to be an ideal visit because of its educational programs, which are designed to be both entertaining and instructive.

Children will love San José's Simón Bolívar Zoo and Botanical Garden, another family-friendly destination. Along with a range of exotic species from across the globe, the zoo is home to a number of local Costa Rican creatures, such as birds, monkeys, and jaguars. The botanical garden offers a lovely backdrop for a leisurely walk and is home to a variety of tropical plants and flowers. The zoo's displays are meant to educate visitors about the animals, their habitats, and the conservation measures being taken to keep them safe. Families visiting the capital city will find the zoo to be a handy stop due to its central location.

Lastly, a trip to Costa Rica wouldn't be complete without a stop to one of its stunning beaches. Numerous beaches around the nation's coastline are ideal for families with kids because they have soft sand, calm waves, and plenty of space for swimming, sandcastle building, and tidal pool exploration. One of Costa Rica's most family-friendly beaches is Playa Conchal, which is situated on the country's northern Pacific coast. The beach is renowned for its fine, white sand composed of small crushed shells and its pristine seas. Young swimmers will love the quiet waters, and snorkeling is fantastic on the neighboring coral reefs.

Playa Manuel Antonio, which is part of Manuel Antonio National Park, is another fantastic beach for kids. This beach provides an amazing backdrop for a day of sunbathing and is encircled by a thick jungle.

Budget-Friendly Hostels and Guesthouses

Travelers from all over the globe are drawn to Costa Rica because it is a dynamic and diversified nation that offers a variety of activities, from experiencing beautiful beaches and lush jungles to learning about rare species and rich cultural legacy. Costa Rica offers a wide range of reasonably priced and pleasant lodging alternatives for those on a tight budget, allowing visitors to take advantage of all the nation has to offer without going over budget. The most well-liked options for tourists looking to save costs without sacrificing an unforgettable and rewarding experience are inexpensive hostels and guesthouses.

Costa Rican hostels are well-known for their warm and inviting ambiance, which makes them a great choice for backpackers, lone travelers, and anybody else hoping to meet people from other countries. Usually created with social interaction in mind, these places provide common rooms like kitchens, lounges, and outdoor areas where visitors may unwind, exchange tales, and meet new people. One of hostels' best features is the feeling of community they create, which makes it possible to meet others who match your interests and exchange advice on how to see Costa Rica.

The cost of hostels is one of its main advantages. The most popular kind of lodging at hostels are dormitory-style rooms, which include bunk beds and communal sleeping arrangements. Because they just pay for a bed instead of a room, travelers may save a lot of money with this arrangement. The size of dorms varies; some may house as little as four individuals, while others can accommodate bigger groups. For extra comfort and security, a lot of hostels now provide rooms exclusively for women. Although dorm rooms are the least expensive choice, many hostels also offer private rooms, which are a little more expensive, to accommodate guests who want more privacy but still want to take advantage of the community aspects of hostel living.

Hostels in Costa Rica often provide a variety of features that improve visitors' entire experience in addition to being reasonably priced. Free Wi-Fi is widely accessible, enabling visitors to plan their trips and remain connected. A simple and affordable way to start the day, many hostels also provide free breakfast, which usually consists of regional food like bread, coffee, and fresh fruit. By planning group activities like guided tours, beach excursions, or social gatherings, some hostels go above and above to provide visitors the chance to experience the local culture and form bonds with other tourists.

Because Costa Rica's hostel sites are as diverse as its surroundings, visitors may choose lodgings that fit their interests and schedule. Hostels are often situated in the heart of important tourist locations, including the capital city of San José, making it simple to get to dining options, transit hubs, and cultural attractions. Hostels in San José are an excellent option to take in the lively atmosphere of the city while saving money for travel to other regions of the nation. Hostels are also widely available in Costa Rica's most isolated and picturesque regions for people who want to get away from it all and experience nature. Hostels provide a starting point for exploring cloud forests, volcanoes, and immaculate beaches in areas like Monteverde, La Fortuna, and the Osa Peninsula. Since many of these hostels include outside areas where visitors may take in views of the jungle, mountains, or ocean, the natural beauty that surrounds them often becomes an essential component of the experience. Travelers may easily go on hikes, animal tours, and other outdoor activities without having to pay a lot of money for transportation or admission fees because of the area's close proximity to national parks and natural reserves.

In Costa Rica, guesthouses provide a more personal and cozy experience than hostels, making them an additional affordable lodging choice. Frequently run by families, guesthouses provide visitors an opportunity to engage with local hosts who are happy to share their local expertise and offer tailored advice. One of the best things about staying in a guesthouse is the personalized touch, which gives visitors a firsthand look at Costa Rican hospitality and an understanding of the local way of life.

In contrast to hostels, guesthouses usually include private rooms, which makes them an excellent choice for families, couples, or tourists who want a more sedate and private environment. Guesthouse rooms are often well equipped with all the essential conveniences for a comfortable stay, despite their simple furnishings. For those who want solitude, guesthouses often also provide private restrooms, which is an extra convenience. Some guesthouses go above and beyond the necessities by providing extra features like cable TV, air conditioning, or even tiny kitchenettes. This makes them an excellent choice for tourists on a tight budget who yet need a little more luxury.

After a day of touring, the typically more casual and laid-back ambiance of guesthouses offers a tranquil haven. In contrast to busy city centers or popular tourist destinations, many guesthouses are situated in residential neighborhoods or rural regions, providing a more tranquil setting. Travelers may appreciate the natural surroundings, engage with people, and get a more true taste of Costa Rican culture in this environment, which enables them to see the country's less touristic and more authentic side.

The chance to eat meals prepared at home is one of the main benefits of staying at a guesthouse. In Costa Rica, a lot of guesthouses provide breakfast in the accommodation charge, and some even let guests order lunch or supper. These dishes give visitors a taste of authentic Costa Rican food since they are often made using local, fresh ingredients. In addition to being a practical choice, dining at the guesthouse offers the opportunity to savor substantial, locally inspired cuisine.

Because they are reasonably priced, guesthouses are a desirable choice for tourists who like to stay comfortably and amicably while still stretching their budget. When compared to hotels or resorts, guesthouses in Costa Rica often provide great value for money, while prices might vary according on location, facilities, and season. Guesthouses in Costa Rica are an affordable option for tourists who like to take their time visiting the nation since they often provide reduced pricing for longer stays.

Compared to bigger, impersonal hotels, staying in a guesthouse offers a more immersive and culturally rich experience in addition to financial savings. Guesthouses are a popular option for tourists who want to engage with the local way of life because of the chance to meet with local hosts and get a taste of Costa Rican daily life. A guesthouse experience adds a level of depth and authenticity to the travel experience, whether it is by engaging in local customs and traditions, talking with the host over breakfast, or receiving advice on the best areas to visit.

In Costa Rica, both hostels and guesthouses have certain benefits that appeal to various kinds of tourists. For those seeking a social and communal experience, hostels are perfect since they allow them to interact with other tourists and take part in group activities. Hostels are an excellent choice for tourists on a tight budget who want to save costs without sacrificing comfort or enjoyment because of their affordable rates. Younger tourists, backpackers, and single travelers who are keen to meet new people and exchange travel stories find hostels' vibrant environment and feeling of community especially alluring.
In contrast, guesthouses provide a more private and personal

experience, which makes them an excellent option for families, couples, or tourists seeking a calmer, more laid-back setting. Guesthouses provide a more immersive experience because of their individualized service and cozy setting, which enables visitors to interact with local hosts and learn about Costa Rican culture. Guesthouses are a popular option for tourists who want to experience Costa Rica's warmth and friendliness without breaking the bank because of their reasonable prices as well as the comfort and convenience they provide.

There are many affordable lodging alternatives available in Costa Rica to suit the requirements and tastes of tourists. You can be certain that you will find pleasant and reasonably priced lodging that will enable you to enjoy Costa Rica's natural beauty and culture without going over budget, whether you decide to stay in a bustling and sociable hostel or a small, quiet guesthouse. For tourists on a tight budget who want to see all Costa Rica has to offer, the country's varied landscapes, abundant wildlife, and welcoming populace make it the perfect location. A hostel or guesthouse is the ideal starting point for an amazing Costa Rican trip, whether you're exploring the local culture, going on an adventure in the jungle, or just lounging on the beach.

Eco-Lodges and Sustainable Stays

Many people consider Costa Rica to be one of the best places in the world for ecotourism, drawing tourists who want to experience the country's natural beauty while also being environmentally conscious and sustainable. Numerous eco-lodges and sustainable lodging options have been built around the nation's varied landscapes, demonstrating its dedication to conservation and responsible tourism. These eco-lodges give travelers a really one-of-a-kind and rewarding vacation experience by allowing them to fully immerse themselves in the natural surroundings while reducing their environmental footprint.

Costa Rican eco-lodges, which are often found in isolated and beautiful locations like jungles, mountains, and coastal regions, are designed to fit in perfectly with their natural environment. These lodges aim to provide a cozy and engaging experience that lets visitors get in touch with nature without sacrificing the environment's purity. This is accomplished via the use of water- and waste-saving techniques, energy-efficient systems, and sustainable construction materials. Through programs like reforestation, habitat restoration, and animal monitoring, many eco-lodges also contribute to conservation efforts, aiming to save the region's ecosystems and fauna.

Eco-lodges in Costa Rica are distinguished by their focus on environmentally friendly architecture and building practices. Locally available materials like bamboo, repurposed wood, and natural stone are often used to build these lodges. This helps to create a feeling of place that reflects the local environment and culture while also lessening the environmental effect of construction. Usually influenced by conventional construction methods, eco-lodges' architecture has buildings that optimize natural light, reduce energy use, and increase ventilation. To further lessen their carbon footprint and dependency on outside resources, several resorts additionally install rainwater collection systems, solar panels, and green roofs.

Beyond the actual buildings, eco-lodges are dedicated to sustainability in all aspects of everyday operations and visitor experiences. For instance, a lot of Costa Rican eco-lodges utilize waste reduction techniques including recycling, composting, and using biodegradable goods. Water conservation is also a top concern, and lodges often use rainwater collecting, greywater systems, and low-flow fixtures to reduce water use. To lessen the environmental effect of food production and transportation, eco-lodges prioritize obtaining foods locally in the kitchen, often from neighboring farms or their own organic gardens. In addition to boosting the local economy, the focus on using organic, locally grown, and fresh products offers visitors a tasty and environmentally friendly dining experience.

In addition to their environmentally friendly operations, Costa Rican eco-lodges provide a variety of experiences and activities that let visitors form deep connections with the natural world. Typical services include wildlife safaris, birding trips, and guided nature walks, which provide visitors the chance to learn about the area animals and plants from experienced guides. Visitors may easily visit some of Costa Rica's most famous natural landscapes since many eco-lodges are situated close to national parks, nature reserves, or protected regions. These eco-friendly and low-impact activities, including trekking through cloud forests, kayaking in mangrove swamps, and snorkeling in coral reefs, guarantee that future generations will be able to appreciate Costa Rica's natural legacy.

The chance to personally assist conservation efforts is one of the main advantages of staying at an eco-lodge. Numerous eco-lodges in Costa Rica are engaged in continuing conservation initiatives, including study on local ecosystems, habitat restoration, and the protection of endangered animals. Visitors to these lodges often have the opportunity to become involved in these programs, whether it's via animal monitoring, tree planting, or community-based conservation efforts. In addition to improving the vacation experience, this active participation helps ensure the region's long-term viability.

The emphasis that Costa Rican eco-lodges have on cultural preservation and community involvement is another significant feature. Numerous lodges engage in close collaboration with their communities, offering jobs, assisting small companies, and fostering cross-cultural interactions. Through events like cooking courses, artisan workshops, and trips to neighboring towns, guests are often invited to learn about the local way of life. In addition to ensuring that the local community benefits from tourism, this focus on cultural sustainability aids in the preservation of the traditional knowledge, practices, and way of life that are essential components of Costa Rica's cultural legacy.

Eco-lodges may be found in a variety of settings, from beautiful beaches to deep jungles, reflecting the diversity of Costa Rica's ecosystems. For instance, eco-lodges on the Osa Peninsula provide a fully immersed experience in one of the world's most biodiverse areas. Corcovado National Park, located on the peninsula, offers visitors the opportunity to explore primary rainforests, see uncommon animals like tapirs and jaguars, and find remote beaches and secret waterfalls. In order to provide a sustainable and cozy haven in the middle of the wilderness, eco-lodges in this area are often constructed with little environmental damage, using natural materials and renewable energy sources.

Eco-lodges in the Monteverde Cloud Forest provide access to one of Costa Rica's most famous natural regions. A wide variety of plant and animal species, including as orchids, bromeliads, and the magnificent quetzal, may be found in the cloud forest's distinctive, chilly, foggy climate. Visitors may enjoy the wonders of the cloud forest while reducing their negative effects on the fragile ecology by booking a room at an eco-lodge in Monteverde. The hotels in this area often provide canopy walks, night treks, and guided tours of the cloud forest, giving guests a thorough and engaging experience of this exceptional setting.

The eco-lodges on the Nicoya Peninsula provide a combination of sustainable living and seaside leisure for visitors wishing to explore Costa Rica's coastal areas. The peninsula is a well-liked location for diving, snorkeling, and surfing because of its stunning beaches, mild seas, and abundant marine life. With open-air buildings, solar energy, and organic gardens that mix in well with the surroundings, eco-lodges in this area are often made to capitalize on the natural environment. While living in lodgings that have an emphasis on sustainability and environmental care, guests may partake in a variety of activities, such as yoga and meditation on the beach or exploring the neighboring mangroves and coral reefs.

Another well-liked ecotourism location is Costa Rica's Caribbean coast, which has eco-lodges that provide a distinctive fusion of beach and jungle settings. For tourists wishing to see a different side of Costa Rica, the area is a great choice because of its Afro-Caribbean culture, abundant wildlife, and relaxed vibe. Eco-lodges in this area often prioritize cultural preservation and community involvement, giving visitors the chance to experience the local way of life via trips to traditional villages, cooking workshops, and dancing lessons. Additionally, the lodges provide visitors access to some of the most stunning natural places in the area, such as Cahuita National Park and the Gandoca-Manzanillo Wildlife Refuge, where they can explore mangrove swamps, coral reefs, and rainforests.

In Costa Rica, eco-lodges and other sustainable lodging options provide a distinctive and enlightening vacation experience that blends comfort, environmental consciousness, and cultural interaction. These lodges are designed to provide visitors a sense of closeness to nature, enabling them to fully appreciate Costa Rica's many ecosystems while reducing their environmental effect. A stay at an eco-lodge offers the chance to enjoy Costa Rica in a sustainable and fulfilling manner, whether you're visiting the beaches of the Nicoya Peninsula, the cloud forests of Monteverde, or the rainforests of the Osa Peninsula.

The local people benefits from tourism, and Costa Rica's natural beauty is preserved for future generations thanks to the focus on conservation, community involvement, and cultural preservation. Eco-lodges and sustainable lodgings are the ideal option for those who are concerned about the environment and want a purposeful and ethical approach to see Costa Rica.

Family-Friendly Accommodations

For families looking for adventure, leisure, and the opportunity to see some of the most varied ecosystems on earth, Costa Rica is a popular choice. There are plenty of lodging options that are tailored to the requirements of families with kids of all ages, and the nation's warm temperature, friendly people, and scenic surroundings make it the perfect destination for family holidays. Costa Rica offers a variety of alternatives to guarantee that families have a pleasant and unforgettable stay, ranging from large resorts with kid-friendly facilities to little guesthouses that give a more private and personal experience.

Families can easily unwind and enjoy their time together thanks to Costa Rica's family-friendly lodging options, which are designed to be both comfortable and convenient. In addition to having features like numerous bedrooms, kitchenettes, and sitting spaces that provide the space and flexibility required for a family holiday, these lodgings often include roomy rooms or suites that can accommodate parents and kids. To make the stay more pleasant for families with little children, several facilities additionally include extra amenities like high chairs, cribs, and childproofing.

When families are selecting lodging, having kid-friendly services and activities is one of the most important factors. Costa Rican hotels and resorts that cater to families often go above and above to make sure that kids have plenty of fun and entertainment alternatives. Kid's clubs are available at many resorts, where kids may engage in games, crafts, and outdoor experiences under adult supervision. These clubs provide parents peace of mind and the chance to unwind alone since they are often manned by qualified experts who are adept at interacting with kids.

Numerous family-friendly lodging options in Costa Rica include a range of outdoor activities that the entire family may enjoy in addition to kid-friendly clubs. Swimming pools are a typical element; many resorts have many pools with shallow sections for little children and water slides for larger ones. For kids who like the water, some resorts even provide water playgrounds or splash pads, which offer limitless entertainment. With facilities like beach chairs, umbrellas, and water sports gear accessible for visitors, beachfront resorts often provide convenient access to the sand and waves for families who enjoy beach time.

Adventure is a major factor in Costa Rica's appeal as a family vacation spot, and the abundance of family-friendly lodging options near the nation's main attractions makes organizing day trips and excursions simple. For instance, homes close to the Arenal Volcano allow quick access to outdoor pursuits like trekking, ziplining, and hot springs, while homes close to Manuel Antonio National Park provide chances for snorkeling, beachcombing, and animal observation. Numerous hotels and resorts provide family-friendly guided tours and excursions with itineraries that consider the interests and demands of young guests.

Costa Rican eco-lodges and nature resorts provide a special chance for families seeking a more immersive experience to get in touch with nature. These lodgings are often found in isolated, unspoiled locations where families may get a close-up look at Costa Rica's biodiversity and natural beauty, such cloud forests, coastal reserves, and rainforests. Children may learn about the local environment, animals, and conservation efforts via the educational programs and activities that eco-lodges often provide. Families may discover and enjoy Costa Rica's natural treasures via guided nature walks, birding excursions, and trips to neighboring national parks.

Small boutique hotels and guesthouses provide a comfortable

and intimate substitute for bigger resorts for families looking for a more laid-back and low-key getaway. With hosts willing to share their local expertise and provide suggestions for family-friendly activities, these lodgings can offer a more personalized experience. Because guesthouses are usually smaller, they might have a cozier, more friendly ambiance that makes it simpler for families to relax and feel comfortable. Family suites or linked rooms are available at many Costa Rican guesthouses, giving families the space and seclusion they want.

Families should also take food choices into account while selecting lodging. Costa Rican hotels and resorts that cater to families often include a variety of eating choices, such as buffet-style restaurants, laid-back cafés, and more formal dining establishments. These restaurants usually provide kid-friendly menus with a wide range of choices to satisfy even the pickiest palates. Many family-friendly hotels also provide room service or in-room dining in addition to on-site dining choices, so families may eat together in the convenience of their own home.

Many lodging establishments in Costa Rica are pleased to fulfill special requests from families with dietary preferences or limitations, such as making vegetarian or gluten-free meals or catering to certain dietary requirements. Families may enjoy a wide variety of tasty and nutritious meals because to Costa Rican cuisine's focus on using local, fresh ingredients. Families may learn how to make traditional Costa Rican meals using local, fresh products by participating in cooking workshops or farm-to-table experiences offered by certain facilities.

Families place a high value on safety and security when selecting lodging, and many Costa Rican family-friendly establishments go above and beyond to make sure their visitors are secure and at ease. This might include having security guards on duty, gated entry, and childproofing rooms. Furthermore, a lot of hotels and resorts provide medical services or collaborate with nearby clinics to give emergency treatment. The employees at these establishments are often educated to meet the requirements of families, helping with anything from making travel arrangements to giving advice on the top destinations to visit with kids.

The comfort and pleasure of a vacation may be significantly impacted by the availability of baby equipment and services for families with young children. Cribs, high chairs, strollers, and baby monitors are available upon request at many Costa Rican family-friendly lodgings, allowing parents to travel light. Additionally, some homes provide babysitter services so that parents may have some alone time knowing their kids are being taken care of.

The location of family-friendly hotels in Costa Rica often provides easy access to local attractions and kid-friendly activities, in addition to the facilities and services offered by the lodgings themselves. For instance, homes close to national parks give the possibility to observe animals, trek through the forest, and find waterfalls, while homes close to the beach offer the chance to make sandcastles, swim, and explore tidal pools. Families may easily explore the region at their own leisure since many family-friendly lodgings also provide transportation services or even set up vehicle rentals.

The variety of lodging alternatives that are available to suit various travel types, tastes, and budgets is one of the best things about taking a family vacation to Costa Rica. You're sure to discover a property that suits your requirements and guarantees a wonderful stay for the entire family, whether you're searching for a rustic eco-lodge that gives an immersive nature experience, a luxury resort with all the conveniences, or a lovely guesthouse that offers a more personal touch.

There are several possibilities for family-friendly lodging in Costa Rica that can accommodate the various demands of families with kids. These lodging options, which range from roomy resorts with kid-friendly features to cozy guesthouses that provide a more individualized experience, are made to guarantee that families can relax, explore, and enjoy their time together in a secure and comfortable environment. Costa Rica is a great place for family holidays because of its stunning natural surroundings, friendly locals, and plenty of facilities and activities. It's the ideal place to form lifelong memories with your loved ones. Costa Rica's family-friendly lodgings provide the ideal foundation for a memorable family vacation, regardless of your preferences for adventure, leisure, or a little bit of both.

Unique Stays

More than only stunning scenery and a wealth of animals can be found in Costa Rica, which also offers a range of distinctive and memorable lodging choices that let visitors completely experience the peace and beauty of the nation. Treehouses, seaside villas, and jungle retreats are among the most unique accommodations available, providing a unique combination of luxury, adventure, and a close connection to nature that is difficult to find elsewhere. These kinds of lodgings are ideal for tourists wanting something different, whether they are searching for adventure, romance, or just a quiet getaway from the commotion of daily life.

Living amid the trees while taking in the views and sounds of the jungle is a really amazing experience when you stay in a treehouse in Costa Rica. In Costa Rica, treehouses are not the straightforward constructions you may remember from your youth; rather, they are often exquisitely crafted and carefully planned to provide comfort and a feeling of adventure. Usually constructed high in the canopy, these treehouses provide breathtaking views of the surrounding forest and give the impression that the occupants are fully in the middle of nature. These treehouses' construction often employs organic materials like bamboo and wood, which fit in well with the surroundings and let the buildings become a part of the scenery.

The feeling of peace and solitude that comes with residing in a treehouse is among its most alluring features. Treehouses provide a tranquil haven away from the bustle and distractions of the outside world, where you may awaken to the sounds of birdsong and the rustle of leaves. Since many of Costa Rica's most recognizable creatures, like monkeys, sloths, and colorful birds, can be seen in the trees, the high location of these lodgings also offers a great opportunity to see wildlife. In a way that few other lodging options can, living in a treehouse allows you to get closer to nature, whether you're sipping your morning coffee on a private balcony, watching the sunset from a hammock, or drifting off to the soothing sounds of the jungle.

Numerous treehouses in Costa Rica have a variety of facilities that improve the whole experience, in addition to their distinctive layout and setting. Even while these treehouses seem secluded and primitive, they often provide contemporary amenities like cozy mattresses, private bathrooms, and even kitchenettes or fully functional kitchens. Some treehouses even include outdoor bathrooms or showers, so you can unwind while taking in the beauty of the surrounding forest and the warm tropical air. Treehouses are a great option for tourists who want to have the best of both worlds because of the harmonious blend of luxury and nature.

Another distinctive and opulent lodging choice in Costa Rica are beachfront villas, which provide the utmost in luxury and leisure along with easy access to the breathtaking coasts of the nation. Usually found on or close to some of Costa Rica's most stunning beaches, these villas provide easy access to the sand and surf as well as expansive views of the ocean. Large windows, open-air living areas, and outdoor terraces enable visitors to completely enjoy the breathtaking vistas and the soft sea breeze. These villas' designs often mirror the natural beauty of their surroundings.

You may take in the ocean's splendor while relaxing in your own private haven when you book a beachfront villa. Imagine spending your days relaxing on the beach, swimming in the warm ocean, or exploring the neighboring tidal pools. You can even imagine waking up to the sound of waves breaking on the coast and watching the dawn over the sea from your terrace. Private pools are another feature of many seaside houses, providing a cool substitute for the ocean and an ideal setting for rest and relaxation. These villas' isolation and solitude make them the perfect option for families wanting a tranquil haven, couples seeking a romantic escape, or anybody wishing to take in the splendor of Costa Rica's coasts in a more private and intimate setting.

Beachfront villas often provide individualized services that are tailored to each visitor's requirements and tastes in addition to their breathtaking settings and opulent facilities. This may include hiring a private chef to create delectable meals with locally sourced, fresh ingredients or hiring a concierge to set up activities like boat trips, surfing, and snorkeling. Your beachfront villa stay will be customized to your preferences thanks to the focus on individualized care, letting you relax and enjoy your trip without worrying about the little things.

Jungle retreats provide a unique and immersive lodging choice that lets you remain in the middle of the rainforest for those who want to really experience Costa Rica's natural splendor. These getaways are often found in isolated, unspoiled locations with a wealth of animals and deep vegetation around them. With constructions made of natural materials and intended to have as little of an effect as possible on the surrounding ecology, jungle retreats usually place an emphasis on sustainability and environmental responsibility.

Reconnecting with nature and distancing oneself from the outer world are two benefits of staying in a jungle retreat. The quiet and isolated location offers the ideal getaway from the pressures of contemporary life, enabling you to rest and revitalize in a tranquil and organic atmosphere. A variety of health activities, including yoga, meditation, and spa treatments, are available at many jungle retreats with the goal of assisting you in finding balance and relaxation. The emphasis on comprehensive well-being and the splendor of the rainforest combine to provide a life-changing experience that leaves you feeling rejuvenated.

Exploring the vast biodiversity of Costa Rica's jungles is one of the best parts of staying at a jungle retreat. Guided nature walks, birdwatching tours, and night hikes are just a few of the activities that allow you to discover the incredible variety of plants and animals that call the rainforest home. Whether you are spotting colorful birds, watching monkeys swing through the trees, or listening to the chorus of frogs at night, the experience of being surrounded by the sights and sounds of the jungle is truly unforgettable.

In addition to their focus on sustainability and wellness, many jungle retreats in Costa Rica also emphasize cultural and community engagement. Guests at these retreats often have the opportunity to learn about the local culture and traditions through activities such as cooking classes, craft workshops, and visits to nearby villages. This emphasis on cultural exchange adds another layer of depth to the experience, allowing you to connect with the people and traditions of Costa Rica in a meaningful way.

The diversity of unique accommodations in Costa Rica, from treehouses and beachfront villas to jungle retreats, offers travelers the chance to experience the country in a way that is both luxurious and deeply connected to the natural environment. Whether you are looking for adventure, relaxation, or a combination of both, these accommodations provide the perfect setting for a truly memorable stay. The combination of comfort, personalized service, and stunning natural surroundings ensures that your time in Costa Rica will be one that you will never forget.

In conclusion, Costa Rica offers a wide range of unique and unforgettable accommodation options that cater to travelers seeking something beyond the ordinary. Whether you are staying in a treehouse high in the rainforest canopy, a luxurious beachfront villa with stunning ocean views, or a serene jungle retreat surrounded by nature, these accommodations provide the perfect balance of luxury, comfort, and connection to the natural world. The emphasis on sustainability, personalized service, and cultural engagement ensures that your stay in Costa Rica is not only enjoyable but also meaningful, allowing you to experience the true beauty and spirit of this incredible country.

CHAPTER 8

GASTRONOMY AND LOCAL CUISINE

Must-Try Costa Rican Dishes

scenery, abundant wildlife, and kind people. But the nation's food is just as fascinating, affording a profound understanding of the people's history, culture, and daily lives. The agricultural legacy of Costa Rica is reflected in its cuisine, which emphasizes simplicity, taste, and nutrition while using fresh, locally produced products. The tastes of Costa Rica are guaranteed to make an impact, whether you're eating at a more upmarket place or at a neighborhood soda, which is a tiny, family-run eatery. Trying the traditional cuisine of the nation is a must-do activity for tourists who want to completely immerse themselves in the local way of life.

Gallo pinto is a morning classic that is adored by both residents and tourists, making it one of Costa Rica's most recognizable meals. Rice and black beans are combined with onions, red bell peppers, cilantro, and a unique sauce known as Salsa Lizano to make the simple yet tasty meal known as gallo pinto. Usually served with tortillas, eggs, cheese, and sometimes fried plantains, the dish makes a filling and substantial breakfast that gives you the energy you need to go through the day. More than simply a food, gallo pinto is a representation of Costa Rican pride and identity. It is a meal that is consumed in families all throughout the nation, and each family adds their own unique touch to the preparation, which often changes somewhat from area to region.

Casado, also known as Costa Rica's national meal, is another food that visitors should not miss. The term "casado," which translates as "married," embodies the concept of combining several ingredients on a single dish. Rice, black beans, a protein (such as chicken, beef, hog, or fish), a salad, and often a side of fried plantains or yucca make up a classic casado. A casado's basic ingredients are made with care and attention to detail, guaranteeing that each component is balanced and tasty. The casado's adaptability makes it a staple in almost every Costa Rican restaurant, from casual roadside cafes to more sophisticated dining venues. This dish, which is often served with a cool cerveza or a refreshing glass of natural fruit juice, offers a genuine flavor of Costa Rican home-cooked meals.

Olla de carne is a popular Costa Rican cuisine that is likely to please everyone who enjoys soups and stews. Chunks of meat, potatoes, carrots, yucca, plantains, and other vegetables are cooked in a tasty broth to create this filling beef stew. Because it takes longer to simmer and allows the flavors to completely emerge, olla de carne is usually made on the weekends or for special occasions. The end product is a warming, nutrient-dense stew that is rich and cozy, ideal for a family get-together or a rainy day. People of all ages, from small toddlers to grandparents, love olla de carne, which is often served with white rice or tortillas on the side.

Arroz with pollo, a tasty rice meal that is often served at parties, family get-togethers, and special occasions, is another well-liked cuisine in Costa Rica. Rice is cooked with shredded chicken, bell peppers, onions, peas, carrots, and a variety of seasonings to make arroz con pollo, or "rice with chicken." A natural red-orange spice called achiote, which gives the rice its vivid color, is often used to color the meal. Usually eaten with a side of salad or fried plantains, arroz con pollo is topped with fresh cilantro. This meal is well-liked for its hearty tastes and adaptability, since it can be readily modified to include other components like vegetables, shrimp, or chorizo.

Rondon is a must-try meal if you want to experience the Caribbean influence in Costa Rican cooking. The traditional fish stew known as "rondón" comes from Costa Rica's Caribbean coast, specifically from the Limón area. A rich and fragrant coconut milk broth is used to prepare a variety of shellfish, including fish, shrimp, and crab. In order to give the stew a deep and fragrant taste, it is usually seasoned with garlic, thyme, cilantro, and a dash of hot chile. Along with fish, root vegetables including yucca, taro, and green plantains are often added to rondón to give the meal structure and heartiness. Both residents and tourists love roondon, a meal that reflects Costa Rica's Afro-Caribbean roots. It's especially good with crusty bread or white rice on the side so you can mop up the flavorful broth.

Another well-liked meal that exemplifies the richness and

inventiveness of Costa Rican cooking is chili. Despite being a relatively recent invention, this meal has already gained popularity among the locals. A white rice foundation is usually topped with seasoned beans, fried pig pieces (chicharrones), fresh pico de gallo (a salsa prepared with tomatoes, onions, cilantro, and lime juice), and avocado slices in a meal known as chifrijo. In order to give a pleasing crunch and a touch of heat, the meal is often topped with tortilla chips and a dab of hot sauce. In pubs and restaurants, chillijo is often served as an appetizer or snack, but it's also substantial enough to be eaten as a full meal. It is a very appealing meal because of its blend of tastes and textures.

Another cuisine that visitors to Costa Rica must taste is ceviche, particularly if they like fish. Fresh raw fish or seafood, such shrimp, is marinated in citrus juice (often lemon or lime) and combined with bell peppers, onions, and cilantro to make ceviche. The fish is "cooked" by the citrus juice's acidity, which gives it a crisp texture and vibrant taste. Ceviche is a light and refreshing meal that is ideal for a hot day. It is often served with tortilla chips, crackers, or fried plantains. There are many distinct kinds of ceviche in Costa Rica, each with its own special variants made with various kinds of fish and other ingredients like coconut or mango. It is a meal that showcases the influence of the coastal areas as well as the quality and freshness of the local ingredients.

Although they may be eaten all year round, tamales are a typical Costa Rican cuisine that are particularly well-liked during the Christmas season. The corn dough used to make tamales is filled with a variety of ingredients, including vegetables, beans, chicken, and pig, and then wrapped in banana leaves and steam-cooked. The ultimate product is a delicious, delicate parcel that is rich in tradition and flavor. Tamales are a sign of festivity and camaraderie as they are often prepared in big quantities and shared with loved ones. The end result is a testament of the love and care that goes into manufacturing tamales, which is a labor-intensive process that often includes many generations working together.

Costa Rica has a wide range of traditional sweets that are guaranteed to please anybody with a sweet taste. Tres leches cake, renowned for its moist and rich texture, is one of the nation's most popular sweets. The light sponge cake used to make tres leches cake is soaked in a concoction of heavy cream, condensed milk, and evaporated milk. After that, the cake is covered with whipped cream and often adorned with cinnamon or fresh fruit. The end product is a sweet, creamy, and completely delightful dessert that is rich and decadent. Tres leches cake is a common option for special events like birthdays and holidays, but it's also available at a lot of bakeries and eateries nationwide.

Arroz con leche, a hearty rice pudding that appeals to all ages, is another classic dish. In order to make arroz con leche, rice is cooked with milk, sugar, and cinnamon until it becomes creamy. The pudding sometimes contains raisins or other dried fruits and is often flavored with vanilla. A simple yet filling dessert that's often served warm, arroz con leche is the ideal treat for a cold evening. This dish has a long history in Costa Rican cooking and is often connected to family get-togethers and early childhood memories.

A significant component of the dining experience, Costa Rica is also renowned for its mouthwatering drinks. A traditional beverage from the Caribbean coast, agua de sapo is prepared with raw cane sugar, ginger, and lime juice. This delightful and exhilarating beverage is ideal for relieving your thirst on a hot day since it is sweet, tangy, and somewhat spicy. Both residents and tourists who like to sample a little bit of the Caribbean love agua de sapo, which is often served chilled.

Another well-liked beverage in Costa Rica is horchata, which is mixed with milk, sugar, cinnamon, and crushed rice or nuts. The drink is pleasant and refreshing, with a smooth and creamy texture and a sweet, somewhat nutty taste. Since horchata is often served with ice, it's the ideal beverage to cool down on a hot day. People of all ages like this beverage, which is often served at restaurants, local markets, and street sellers.

The agricultural background, cultural influences, and dedication to using only locally obtained and fresh ingredients are all reflected in Costa Rican cuisine, which provides a wide variety of meals. There is something for every pallet, from filling breakfast mainstays like gallo pinto to tasty main courses like casado and arroz con pollo, and from light seafood selections like ceviche to decadent sweets like tres leches cake. Costa Rican cuisine is certain to make an impact, whether you are eating at a more upmarket restaurant or a neighborhood café. Any trip to Costa Rica must include sampling the cuisine, which offers a delectable and genuine sample of the customs and culture that make this nation so unique.

Best Restaurants in San José

The vibrant capital of Costa Rica, San José, is a center of the country's economy and culture and provides tourists with a wide range of activities. The city's eating scene, one of its numerous attractions, is a lively and varied display of Costa Rican culture and foreign influences. San José has a large selection of restaurants that suit all interests and preferences, whether you're a gourmet trying to sample regional cuisine or a tourist searching for an unforgettable dining experience. The city is a must-visit location for anybody interested in Costa Rican cuisine because of its diverse culinary scene, which reflects the city's history, geography, and the inventiveness of its chefs.

Grano de Oro, housed in the opulent Hotel Grano de Oro, is one of San José's most renowned dining establishments. This restaurant is well-known for combining French and Costa Rican cooking, providing a menu that is both elegant and rich in regional customs. With its traditional furnishings, soft lighting, and a lovely outdoor terrace, Grano de Oro exudes a cozy and welcoming atmosphere that is ideal for a special event or a romantic evening. From delicate meats and fresh seafood to locally produced vegetables and herbs, the menu offers a range of meals that showcase the finest of Costa Rican products. Costa Rican Coffee Crusted Tenderloin, a flawlessly cooked steak imbued with the rich tastes of Costa Rican coffee, and Grano de Oro Salad, which blends mixed greens with tropical fruits and a tangy vinaigrette, are two of the restaurant's signature dishes. With wines from both the Old and New Worlds, the restaurant's comprehensive wine list is the ideal accompaniment to any meal. The Tres Leches Cake, which adds a sweet and creamy conclusion to a memorable meal, is a must-try dessert.

Le Monastère, a French-inspired restaurant with stunning city views from its hilltop setting, is another popular dining place in San José. The restaurant's location, which is a former monastery, is distinctive and evocative, with its stone walls, stained glass windows, and candlelight dining rooms lending an air of vintage beauty. Le Monastère's menu is a celebration of French cooking, with everything from traditional fare like foie gras and escargot to more modern dishes made with regional ingredients. The restaurant's beautifully prepared steaks, which are presented with a choice of sauces and accompaniments and are grilled to perfection, are especially well-known. A collection of excellent wines from France and other well-known wine areas may be found in the magnificent wine cellar of Le Monastère. Le Monastère is a well-liked option for both residents and tourists seeking an unforgettable dining experience because of its delicious cuisine, breathtaking views, and romantic ambiance.

La Esquina de Buenos Aires provides a genuine taste of Costa Rica's culinary legacy with a dash of Argentine flare for those who want to experience traditional Costa Rican food. Popular with both residents and visitors, this vibrant restaurant is situated in the center of San José. From robust grilled meats and fresh seafood to delectable stews and soups, the menu offers a range of meals that highlight Costa Rican cuisine. The Churrasco, a flavorful grilled steak topped with chimichurri sauce and accompanied by roasted potatoes and grilled veggies, is one of the restaurant's specialties. In addition, the restaurant serves a variety of traditional drinks like the Pisco Sour and Argentine wines, which go well with the dish's savory and rich ingredients. La Esquina de Buenos Aires is a must-visit for anybody wishing to experience the warmth and friendliness of Costa Rican dining because of its lively ambiance, welcoming staff, and hearty meals.

Restaurante Silvestre, a sophisticated restaurant that serves a contemporary twist on traditional Costa Rican cuisine, is another noteworthy establishment in San José. Silvestre, housed in a tastefully renovated colonial home, blends modern culinary techniques with the allure of historic San José. The restaurant's menu features dishes that showcase Costa Rica's rich agricultural legacy and the culinary innovation of its chefs, drawing inspiration from the country's different regions. Every dish is expertly prepared to highlight the tastes, textures, and hues of regional ingredients, creating a visually spectacular and delectably fulfilling dining experience. From savory appetizers to rich sweets, the restaurant's tasting menu lets patrons sample a range of meals. Highlights include the Chicharrón de Pulpo, a crispy octopus dish with a tart tamarind sauce, and the Tico

Ceviche, which is created with fresh fish marinated in citrus liquids and served with avocado and plantain chips. Additionally, the restaurant serves a wide variety of creative cocktails, many of which are made using regional fruits and herbs to give traditional concoctions a distinctive touch.

In the center of San José, Tierra Gaucha Parrilla Argentina provides a genuine Argentine dining experience for a taste of worldwide tastes. Asado, or Argentine-style grilled meats, are the specialty of this well-known eatery. They are prepared over an open flame and offered with a range of traditional accompaniments. A large variety of steaks, sausages, and other meats are available on the menu; they are all carefully cooked by the restaurant's talented chefs using only the best sources. The Bife de Chorizo, a well cooked, thick, and meaty steak topped with chimichurri sauce, is one of Tierra Gaucha's best meals. Along with a carefully chosen wine list that features some of the greatest wines from Argentina's well-known vineyards, the restaurant serves a variety of empanadas, salads, and other Argentine favorites. Tierra Gaucha is a well-liked option for both informal meals and special events because of its cozy and welcoming ambiance, delectable cuisine, and attentive service.

A well-liked local institution that has been dishing up traditional Costa Rican cuisine for decades, Soda Tapia is a great choice for those seeking a more relaxed dining experience. This simple restaurant, which is close to La Sabana Park, provides a taste of real Costa Rican comfort cuisine in a laid-back atmosphere. The menu offers a number of traditional meals, including arroz con pollo, casado, and gallo pinto, all of which are prepared using ingredients that are obtained locally and presented in substantial servings. The restaurant is especially well-known for its substantial breakfasts, which include a range of dishes such fresh fruit, tortillas, and scrambled eggs. Popular with both residents and visitors, Soda Tapia is a must-visit for anybody wishing to enjoy Costa Rican cuisine in a relaxed and inviting setting because of its excellent food, reasonable rates, and helpful staff.

Another excellent place to eat in San José is Bacchus, which serves a chic and modern fusion of Italian and Mediterranean food. Bacchus, which is situated in the posh Santa Ana area, is well-known for its tasty and fresh food that is prepared with premium ingredients and presented with style and flair. Along with grilled meats, wood-fired pizzas, and pasta dishes, the menu also offers vegetarian and seafood selections. Risotto al Funghi, a rich and creamy risotto cooked with Parmesan cheese and wild mushrooms, is one of the restaurant's specialties. Along with a wide range of handmade cocktails and artisanal brews, Bacchus also has a comprehensive wine list that includes options from Italy, Spain, and other well-known wine areas. Bacchus is a well-liked option for both informal meals and important occasions because of its clean and contemporary design, superb cuisine, and first-rate service.

With an emphasis on sustainable and fresh seafood, Restaurante Tin Jo provides a distinctive blend of Asian and

Latin American tastes for seafood enthusiasts. For more than 40 years, this unique restaurant in the center of San José has been offering creative and delectable food. Thai curries, Japanese sushi, Peruvian ceviche, and Costa Rican seafood delicacies are just a few of the items on the menu, which celebrates the many culinary traditions of Asia and Latin America. The Pad Thai, a traditional Thai noodle dish prepared with shrimp, tofu, peanuts, and a zesty tamarind sauce, is one of Restaurante Tin Jo's best dishes. Along with a range of vegetarian and vegan alternatives, the restaurant serves sashimi, sushi rolls, and other Japanese classics. Restaurante Tin Jo is a popular among both residents and tourists because of its lively and colorful atmosphere, mouthwatering cuisine, and friendly staff.

There is something for every taste and inclination in San José's vibrant and varied food scene. Foodies may choose from a variety of selections at the city's restaurants, which provide both international and traditional Costa Rican cuisine. San José offers plenty to offer whether you're planning a special occasion, a romantic evening, or a laid-back lunch with friends. The city's rich cultural legacy, dedication to using only the freshest, most locally obtained foods, and the inventiveness and enthusiasm of its chefs are all reflected in its culinary scene. Dining in San José is an experience that is certain to make an impact and give you a better knowledge of the nation's customs and culture, regardless of how experienced you are as a tourist.

Food Markets and Street Eats

In Costa Rica, food is a rich and colorful aspect of daily life rather than only a source of nourishment. Exploring the country's vibrant food markets and trying its street cuisine is the best method for those who want to fully appreciate its tastes and culture. Both residents and tourists may enjoy traditional meals, locally sourced food, and the kind, inviting ambiance that Costa Rica is renowned for at these locations, which provide a genuine experience of Costa Rican living. The spirit of Costa Rican cuisine is brought to life in the food markets and street sellers, offering a multisensory experience that is as much about the locals and their culture as it is about the food.

The capital city of San José's Mercado Central is one of Costa Rica's most recognizable food marketplaces. Founded in 1880, this market is a maze of stands and merchants offering a wide range of goods, from traditional Costa Rican cuisine and handicrafts to fresh vegetables and meats. You are instantly engrossed in the sights, sounds, and scents of Costa Rican culture as you stroll through the busy aisles of Mercado Central. The smell of sizzling meats, spices, and new coffee fills the air as sellers shout their products to onlookers. Locals visit the market to buy their daily supplies, meet up with friends, and get a quick dinner at one of the numerous food booths, making it a microcosm of Costa Rican life.

A variety of tasty and reasonably priced traditional Costa

Rican foods are available at Mercado Central. A thick and savory seafood soup cooked with a variety of fresh fish, shrimp, and other shellfish, boiled in a broth with tomatoes, onions, garlic, and cilantro, is one of the most well-liked dishes. In order to balance the intense tastes of the seafood, this filling soup is often served with a side of rice and a slice of lime. Arroz con leche, a hearty rice pudding mixed with milk, sugar, cinnamon, and sometimes raisins, is another must-try item at the market. Locals love this sweet delight, which they often consume for dessert or as a midmorning snack.

Mercado Central is an excellent spot to try fresh tropical fruits, many of which may be unknown to tourists, in addition to the prepared cuisine. From luscious mangoes and delicious pineapples to more unusual choices like guanábana (soursop) and mamón chino (rambutan), Costa Rica is renowned for its wide variety and abundance of fruits. For those who want to learn more about the local produce, the market is an enjoyable and instructive experience since the merchants are often more than eager to provide samples and describe the various fruit varieties.

A short distance from Mercado Central is Mercado Borbón, another well-known food market in San José. With an emphasis on fresh fruit, meats, and seafood, Mercado Borbón provides an equally rich gastronomic experience while being smaller and less crowded. This market is well-known for having a large variety of fresh fish and shellfish, which makes it a fantastic spot to try some of the prepared seafood meals or buy components for a home-cooked dinner. The ceviche stalls, where merchants make fresh ceviche in front of you by combining marinated fish or shrimp with lime juice, cilantro, onions, and peppers, are one of the attractions of Mercado Borbón. The end product is a spicy and refreshing meal that's ideal for a light lunch or a fast snack.

Outside of the markets, Costa Rica's street food culture provides more insight into the nation's gastronomic customs. In addition to being tasty, street food in Costa Rica is an inexpensive and practical option to eat while on the road. A wide range of traditional foods, often made fresh to request, are sold by street vendors and little food booths around the nation. Empanadas, delicious pastries stuffed with cheese, beans, pork, or potatoes, are among the most popular street meals in Costa Rica. These portable delights are often eaten for breakfast or as a midday snack since they're ideal for a quick nibble.

Chifrijo, a meal that blends the greatest Costa Rican ingredients in one bowl, is another well-liked street snack. A rice and bean foundation is usually topped with avocado slices, fresh pico de gallo (a salsa prepared with tomatoes, onions, and cilantro), and chicharrones (crispy fried pork). You may adjust the dish's taste and degree of spiciness to your preference since it's often served with tortilla chips and a side of spicy sauce. Chifrijo is a satisfying and tasty meal that perfectly captures the simplicity and heartiness of Costa Rican cooking.

Without discussing tamales, a typical meal that is particularly well-liked during the Christmas season but is available year-round at street booths and markets, no discussion about Costa Rican street cuisine would be complete. A combination of pork, chicken, beans, and vegetables are stuffed into corn dough to make tamales, which are then wrapped in banana leaves and steam-cooked. The ultimate product is a delicious, delicate parcel that is rich in tradition and flavor. Tamales are a wonderful way to sample the cozy and homely tastes of Costa Rican cuisine and are often eaten as a snack or light dinner.

Seafood-focused street cuisine is common in coastal communities, where sellers serve meals that emphasize the quality and freshness of the local catch. Patacones con ceviche is one such meal that combines a plate of fresh ceviche with crispy fried green plantains. The acidic, refreshing ceviche and the crunchy, salty patacones combine to provide the ideal harmony of tastes and textures. Due to the quantity of fresh fish, this meal is especially well-liked along the Pacific and Caribbean coastlines, where it is a mainstay of the local street food scene.

Costa Rican street cuisine also provides a range of traditional sweets and snacks that are guaranteed to please anybody with a sweet appetite. A common street food treat, churros are fried dough pastries coated in sugar and often consumed with coffee or hot chocolate. These crunchy and sweet sweets are ideal for a late-night treat or as a snack in the day. Cajeta de coco, a sweet coconut candy prepared with sugar, condensed milk, and shredded coconut, is another well-liked snack. The creamy, chewy, and intensely coconut-flavored cajeta de coco is gratifying and irresistible.

Exploring Costa Rica's food markets and street food is a journey of connection and discovery that goes beyond the cuisine itself. The markets serve as gathering spaces for people to share tales, trade recipes, and enjoy the tastes of their culture in addition to being locations to purchase food. The vendors are proud of their goods and are always willing to share their expertise and enthusiasm with clients. Many of them have been in the markets for decades. Going to a food market in Costa Rica is an immersive experience that provides a profound and genuine understanding of the nation's culinary legacy, whether you are trying a new fruit, seeing a seller create a traditional meal, or just taking in the lively scene.

In a similar vein, Costa Rica's street food culture reflects the nation's enjoyment of tasty, fresh, and basic ingredients. Using recipes that have been handed down through the years, the meal is often cooked with care and attention to detail. In addition to sating your appetite, eating street food in Costa Rica allows you to interact with the locals, experience daily life, and have a greater understanding of the culture that surrounds the cuisine.

Any traveler wishing to really immerse themselves in Costa Rican culture must taste the rich and diverse gastronomic experience that the country's food markets and street cuisine have to offer. These locations provide a genuine experience of Costa Rican culture, from the busy streets of Mercado Central to the little street vendors offering ceviche and empanadas. The nation's agricultural past and enjoyment of straightforward, honest cooking are reflected in the food's freshness, taste, and rich tradition. Exploring Costa Rica's food markets and street food is a journey that is guaranteed to leave you with enduring memories and a greater awareness of the country's lively and diversified culinary scene, regardless of your level of experience with food.

Cooking Classes and Culinary Tours

Travelers may enjoy a multitude of activities in Costa Rica, from taking in its lively culture to discovering its varied landscapes and abundant wildlife. Costa Rican food, which is ingrained in the history, geography, and agricultural methods of the nation, is among the most fulfilling ways to engage with its culture. Cooking lessons and culinary tours provide an interesting and instructive experience for those who want to explore the methods, ingredients, and customs that make Costa Rican cuisine distinctive rather than just sampling the local cuisine.

With the help of experienced chefs or local cooks who are passionate about the nation's culinary legacy, tourists may take cooking lessons in Costa Rica to learn how to make traditional meals using fresh, local products. More than just teaching you how to cook, these classes give you the chance to learn about the cultural significance of food in Costa Rican culture, how agriculture shapes the country's diet, and how to bring back new recipes and skills that will help you recreate Costa Rican flavors long after your trip is over.

Traditional meals like gallo pinto, casado, and arroz con pollo are the topic of one of the most well-liked kinds of cooking lessons in Costa Rica. Often regarded as Costa Rica's national meal, gallo pinto is a simple yet tasty dish made of rice and black beans cooked with onions, peppers, and a unique sauce known as Salsa Lizano. The preparation of the sautéed veggies and spices that give gallo pinto its unique taste may come after learning how to correctly prepare the rice and beans in a standard culinary lesson. The creation of side dishes like fried plantains, eggs, or tortillas that are often eaten with gallo pinto may also be covered in the session. Participants get an understanding of the methods required to prepare these meals as well as a respect for the harmony of tastes and textures that characterize Costa Rican cooking via practical experience.

Another mainstay of Costa Rican cooking is casado, which combines a number of ingredients on one plate, such as rice, beans, a protein like fish or chicken, a salad, and often fried plantains or yucca. In order to teach participants about the many kinds of beans, vegetables, and meats that are often used in Costa Rican cuisine, a casado-focused cooking class can start with a trip to the local market. The teacher may go over how to choose the best ingredients and how to cook each part of the meal, from seasoning the meat to perfectly cooking the rice and beans. In addition to having made a whole dinner at the conclusion of the session, participants have learned how each component of the dish adds to the overall harmony of tastes.

Some cooking workshops provide the chance to learn about regional specialties and lesser-known recipes for individuals who want to experience the variety of Costa Rican cuisine. For instance, attendees could learn how to make rondón, a typical seafood stew cooked with coconut milk, fish, and root vegetables, on Costa Rica's Caribbean coast. The use of regional herbs and spices that give the meal its distinct taste, as well as methods for cooking with coconut milk, may be covered in the lesson. In other areas, participants might learn how to prepare tamales, a year-round favorite that is particularly well-liked during the Christmas season. In order to make tamales, maize dough stuffed with beans, chicken, or pig is wrapped in banana leaves and steamed until it becomes soft. A demonstration of how to make the corn dough, fill and wrap the tamales, and steam them to get the ideal texture could all be included in a tamale-focused cooking lesson.

In addition to cooking lessons, Costa Rican culinary tours provide visitors the opportunity to delve further into the nation's gastronomic culture. A behind-the-scenes look at the procedures involved in getting Costa Rican foods from the field to the table is offered by these trips, which often include visits to nearby farms, markets, and food producers. A culinary tour may, for instance, transport guests to a coffee farm, where they can see the growing and harvesting of coffee beans, learn about Costa Rica's coffee industry history, and sample several coffee varietals. A visit to a sugarcane farm may also be included of the trip, where guests may see the production of sugar and learn how to make tapa de dulce, a traditional unrefined sugar that is a staple in many Costa Rican delicacies.

One of Costa Rica's most well-known products, chocolate, is the subject of another well-liked kind of culinary trip. These excursions are often held at cacao farms, where visitors may see the harvesting and processing of cacao beans, learn about the history of cacao farming in Costa Rica, and take part in a hands-on workshop to create their own chocolate. A taste of several chocolate varieties may also be included of the tour, giving attendees a chance to sample the whole spectrum of flavors that may be produced using various ingredients and processing methods.

Some culinary excursions provide the chance to visit organic farms and discover sustainable agricultural methods for individuals who are interested in learning more about Costa Rica's farm-to-table movement. A trip around the farm's fields, where visitors may see the cultivation of various crops, get knowledge about composting and soil management, and even take part in the harvest of seasonal fruits and vegetables, may be a component of these excursions. A farm-to-table dinner, where guests may savor meals prepared using the fresh, organic products they assisted in harvesting, may be served at the tour's conclusion. This kind of trip offers a greater respect for the labor that goes into creating premium, sustainable foods as well as a better knowledge of the relationship between the land and the food.

For individuals who want to learn more about certain facets of Costa Rica's culinary culture, the nation offers additional specialized experiences in addition to standard cooking lessons and culinary tours. A crucial component of Costa Rican cuisine, salsas y condimentos, or sauces and condiments, are the subject of certain seminars and excursions. In addition to other traditional condiments like chilero (pickled vegetables) and chimichurri (a sauce made with parsley, garlic, and vinegar), participants may learn how to prepare the famous Costa Rican sauce, salsa lizano. These courses often stress how crucial it is to balance tastes and how condiments may improve a dish's overall flavor.

A lesson or tour that focuses on traditional Costa Rican sweets is another specialized experience. Participants might learn how to create arroz con leche, a hearty rice pudding with vanilla and cinnamon flavors, or tres leches cake, a rich and creamy dessert prepared with three kinds of milk. Other traditional candies like melcochas, a kind of sugar candy prepared from tapa de dulce, or cajeta de coco, a coconut candy, may also be covered in the session. A gastronomic adventure through Costa Rican cuisine comes to a delightful finale with these events, which also provide participants the chance to take home recipes they may make for their loved ones.

Some cooking lessons and tours in Costa Rica are designed to be engaging and enjoyable for those who want a more relaxed and sociable culinary experience. They often conclude with a group supper where guests may share in the results of their hard work. A typical Costa Rican house or an outdoor cooking area where participants may learn how to cook over an open fire or in a wood-fired oven may serve as the setting for these activities. There are many of chances to chat, ask questions, and share experiences while dining with new people in a laid-back and friendly setting.

Travelers may explore Costa Rica's culture, history, and culinary traditions in a unique and fascinating manner by taking cooking lessons and culinary tours. Learning how to prepare traditional foods like tamales and gallo pinto, investigating the farm-to-table movement, or mastering the craft of chocolate making all provide a profound and genuine connection to Costa Rican cuisine. In addition to giving participants a deeper understanding of the components, methods, and cultural importance of Costa Rican food, the experiential aspect of these seminars and excursions enables them to acquire useful skills and information that they can carry back with them. Cooking lessons and culinary tours in Costa Rica are an amazing opportunity to see the heart and soul of this stunning nation for anybody with an interest in food, culture, and travel.

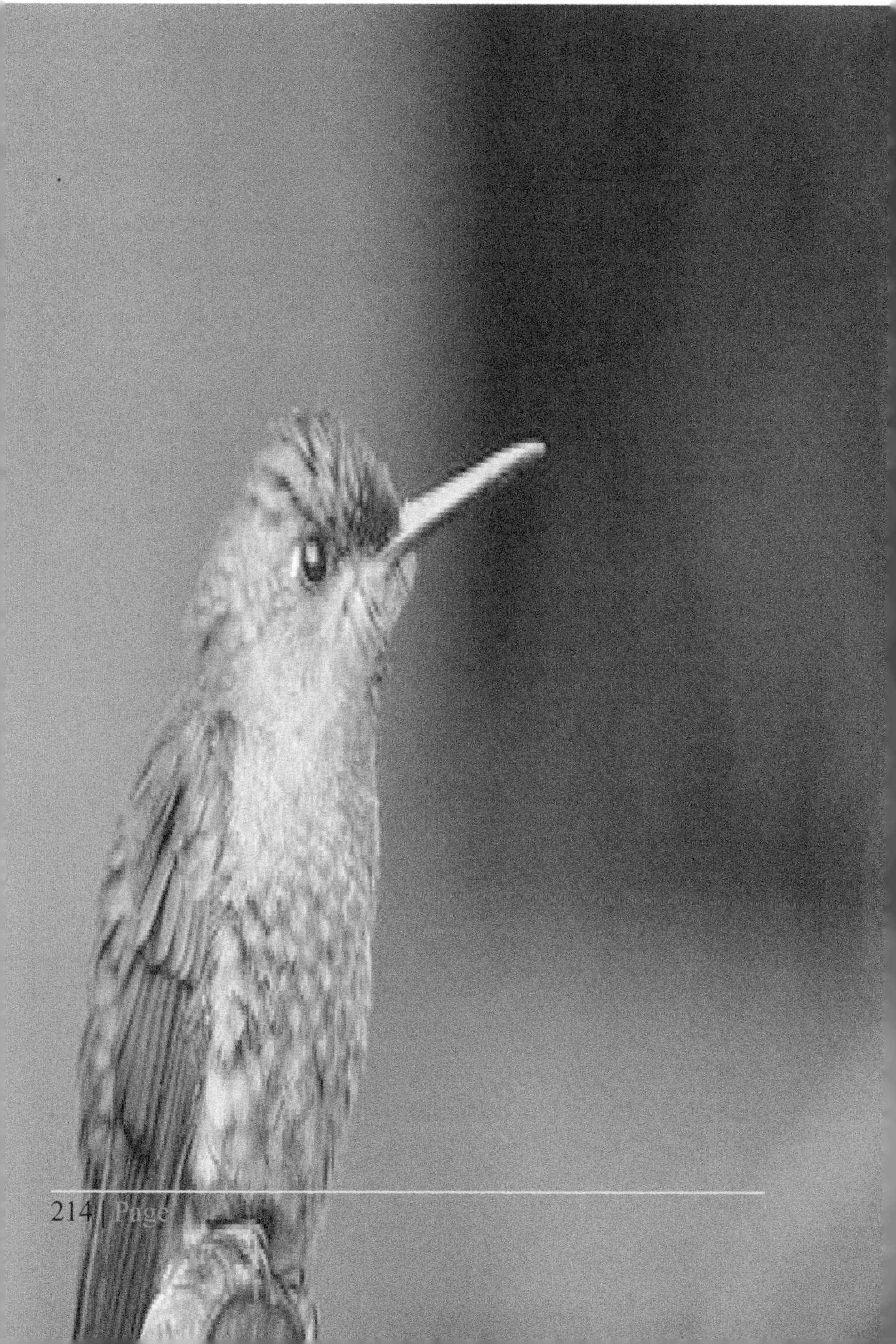

CHAPTER 9

CULTURAL AND HISTORICAL INSIGHTS

Indigenous Cultures and Traditions

Costa Rica is renowned for its lively culture, abundant wildlife, and stunning scenery. Costa Rica's indigenous customs and traditions are another facet of the country that is intricately knit into the fabric of its character, even though tourists often concentrate on its natural beauty and ecotourism prospects. The rich history of Costa Rica's indigenous peoples extends back thousands of years before European immigrants arrived, and their cultural legacy is still a vital component of the nation's identity today. Exploring the indigenous cultures and customs gives a special and meaningful opportunity to connect with the land and its people for those who want to understand Costa Rica beyond its beaches and jungles.

Numerous indigenous communities, each with its own unique language, culture, and way of life, call Costa Rica home. The Bribri, Cabécar, Maleku, Ngäbe, Boruca, Térraba, Chorotega, and Huetar are some of these ethnogroups. Many of these groups have managed to transmit down their cultural customs, dialects, and practices from one generation to the next in spite of the difficulties posed by colonialism and modernity. Visiting these villages and learning about their customs provides a unique chance for tourists interested in cultural immersion to acquire understanding of a long-standing and ancient way of life.

The Bribri people are one of Costa Rica's most well-known indigenous communities; they mostly live in the Talamanca area, which is close to the Caribbean coast. The Bribri have a strong connection with the earth, and agriculture—especially the production of cacao, which has long been a mainstay of their nutrition and economy—is deeply ingrained in their culture. Cacao is more than simply a crop to the Bribri; it has spiritual meaning and is used in many ceremonies and rituals. In addition to learning about the spiritual significance of cacao in Bribri culture, visitors may discover the ancient techniques of cacao production and processing in Bribri villages. Numerous Bribri families welcome travelers into their homes and provide guided tours of their farms, allowing guests to take part in the harvesting and processing of cacao and taste the rich, chocolaty beverage that the Bribri have been drinking for centuries.

The Bribri are renowned for their traditional medicine, which is founded on a profound comprehension of nature and the therapeutic qualities of plants, in addition to their farming methods. The Bribri are well-versed in the therapeutic applications of regional plants, and their shamans, referred to as awa, are adept at treating a variety of illnesses using herbs. Meeting with an awa and learning about the several plants used in traditional medicine, as well as the customs and traditions related to healing, may be an opportunity for visitors to Bribri villages. This facet of Bribri culture emphasizes the significance of maintaining traditional knowledge in the face of contemporary problems, as well as the intimate connection between the people and the natural environment.

The Boruca people, who reside in the southern part of Costa Rica, close to the Panamanian border, are another indigenous community with a rich cultural legacy. Perhaps the most well-known aspect of the Boruca is their elaborate and colorful masks, which are worn at the yearly Fiesta de los Diablitos (Festival of the Little Devils). The Boruca's resistance to Spanish colonialism is reenacted at this event, which occurs between the end of December and the beginning of January. The ancestors' spirits and the natural environment are symbolized by the masks, which are hand-carved from balsa wood and painted in vivid, striking hues. Men wearing these masks participate in fictitious conflicts with characters that symbolize the Spanish invaders during the celebration, signifying the Boruca people's tenacity and will to maintain their tradition.

The mask-making process, a labor-intensive and highly skilled trade that has been handed down through the years, is something that visitors visiting Boruca villages may learn about. The strong bond between the Boruca people and their surroundings is reflected in the artists' frequent use of natural aspects into their creations, such as legendary beings, plants, and animals. The Boruca are renowned for their textile skills, especially the weaving of vibrant textiles on ancient looms, in addition to their mask-making. These textiles often include elaborate patterns and motifs that narrate tales of the cultural beliefs and history of the Boruca people. A visit to a Boruca village provides a unique chance for anyone interested in indigenous art and handicraft to see these customs in action and to contribute to the conservation of this significant cultural legacy.

Another indigenous community that has preserved much of its ancient methods of life is the Cabécar people, who reside in the isolated highlands of the Talamanca area. The profound spirituality of the Cabécar is well-known and stems from their conviction that all living things are interrelated. In order to preserve peace between the people, the land, and the spiritual realm, ceremonies and rituals are led by their spiritual leaders, or usékar, who are essential members of the community. An essential component of their cultural identity is the Cabécar language, one of Costa Rica's oldest and most intricate indigenous languages. Efforts are being undertaken to conserve and revive the language among the next generation.

Due to its distant position, it might be difficult for tourists to get to the Cabécar settlements, but those who do so are rewarded with a unique and genuine cultural experience. The Cabécar live in tiny, dispersed communities, often in traditional ranchos—thatch and wood-framed homes. Because they depend on farming, hunting, and gathering for their survival, these communities are essentially self-sufficient. In addition to learning about the spiritual importance of the natural environment in Cabécar culture, visitors may discover the traditional farming, fishing, and weaving methods used by Cabécar people. A significant perspective on the significance of conserving cultural and natural legacy may be gained from the Cabécar way of life, which provides a look into a civilization that has mostly escaped contemporary influences.

Another indigenous community with a strong cultural legacy is the Maleku, who reside in the northern part of Costa Rica, close to the Arenal Volcano. The Maleku are renowned for their dedication to protecting the environment and their profound regard for nature. They have a strong heritage of environmental care, which is seen in their hunting customs, farming methods, and utilization of natural resources. They also believe that spirits inhabit the natural world. In addition, the Maleku are well-known for their traditional dance and song, which are significant aspects of their spiritual and cultural lives. In addition to seeing holy locations and natural regions that have special meaning for the Maleku people, visitors may take part in cultural excursions that include performances of traditional dance, music, and storytelling.

There are several additional indigenous communities in Costa Rica, each with its own distinct customs, dialects, and lifestyles, in addition to these particular indigenous tribes. Living in the northwest of Guanacaste, the Chorotega are renowned for their pottery, which is created using age-old methods that go all the way back to pre-Columbian times. The southern Pacific people known as the Ngäbe are renowned for their elaborate and vibrant beading, which is used to make jewelry, clothes, and other ornaments. The southern Puntarenas is home to the Térraba, who are renowned for their traditional farming methods as well as their attempts to maintain their language and cultural customs.

There are many chances for visitors who want to learn more about Costa Rica's indigenous cultures to interact with these groups in a meaningful and respectful manner. To teach tourists about their customs, history, and way of life, several indigenous organizations provide cultural excursions and experiences. In addition to showing off traditional crafts, music, and dancing, these excursions sometimes involve visits to traditional houses, farms, and workshops. Visitors may learn more about Costa Rica's cultural variety and the significance of indigenous groups to the nation's legacy by taking part in these events.

Given that indigenous communities in Costa Rica, like indigenous peoples worldwide, have encountered tremendous obstacles in maintaining their customs and way of life, it is critical to approach these cultural experiences with respect and an open mind. Land rights, access to healthcare and education, and the effects of globalization and industrialization are among the problems that many of these communities still face. Travelers may help guarantee that these significant cultural practices are preserved and passed on to future generations by supporting indigenous-led cultural projects and tourist programs.

A rich and priceless perspective on Costa Rica's history, identity, and connection with nature may be gained from its indigenous cultures and customs. Every indigenous group in Costa Rica has a distinct cultural heritage that is worth discovering and comprehending, from the Bribri's close ties to cacao and traditional medicine to the Boruca's colorful mask-making and textile work, the Cabécar's spiritual practices, and the Maleku's environmental stewardship. Interacting with these indigenous communities offers tourists looking to develop a closer relationship with Costa Rica and its people the chance to discover, contemplate, and appreciate the variety and resiliency of the human spirit.

Museums, Art Galleries, and Cultural Centers

Costa Rica is a nation renowned for its rich biodiversity, immaculate beaches, and lush jungles, but it also has a thriving cultural scene that reflects its many influences and complicated past. There are several museums, art galleries, and cultural institutions in Costa Rica that provide visitors interested in learning more about the country's creative and cultural legacy a comprehensive and nuanced view of its history, present, and future. By providing information on anything from pre-Columbian civilizations to modern art and cultural manifestations, these institutions act as windows into Costa Rica's identity. A visit to these locations is a must for everyone interested in learning about Costa Rica's cultural landscape.

The Museo Nacional de Costa Rica (National Museum of Costa Rica), which is situated in the capital city of San José, is one of the most well-known cultural establishments in Costa Rica. The museum offers a thorough overview of Costa Rican history from pre-Columbian times to the present and is housed in a historic structure that was once a military barracks. Starting with the earliest human settlements in the area and moving through the many eras of Costa Rican history, the museum's exhibits are organized chronologically. Numerous relics that provide insight into the life of the indigenous peoples who lived the region long before European immigrants arrived may be explored by visitors, such as ceramics, gold jewelry, and stone tools.

Its collection of pre-Columbian gold items, housed in a special exhibit called the Sala de Oro, is one of the centerpieces of the Museo Nacional. These elaborate and exquisitely made artifacts provide insight into the artistic and spiritual customs of Costa Rica's prehistoric societies, many of which were used in religious and ceremonial settings. Exhibits on the colonial era, the fight for independence, and the evolution of Costa Rican society in the 19th and 20th centuries are also available at the museum. The Museo Nacional is a vibrant and constantly changing cultural attraction because, in addition to its historical displays, it also holds temporary exhibitions on a range of subjects, from natural history to contemporary art.

The Museo del Oro Precolombino (Pre-Columbian Gold Museum), which is situated in San José, is another significant cultural organization in Costa Rica. The goal of this museum, which is a division of the Central Bank Museums, is to preserve and exhibit Costa Rica's extensive pre-Columbian goldwork heritage. More than 1,600 gold jewelry pieces, sculptures, and ceremonial items—many of which are over a millennium old—are part of the museum's collection. In addition to being exquisite works of art, the items on exhibit provide important insights about the customs, beliefs, and social systems of the ancient peoples of Costa Rica.

The zoomorphic pendants, which are tiny, finely sculpted gold sculptures that depict animals like crocodiles, jaguars, and birds, are especially well-known from the Museo del Oro. These pendants are said to have had deep spiritual and symbolic significance and were often worn as amulets. The displays in the museum also look at the methods that ancient goldsmiths used, such as engraving, hammering, and casting, as well as the networks of commerce that linked Costa Rica to other parts of Central and South America. The Museo del Oro provides an engrossing and comprehensive examination of one of Costa Rica's most important cultural legacies for tourists interested in archaeology and ancient art.

The Museo de Arte Costarricense (Costa Rican Art Museum) in San José is a must-see location for anybody interested in modern art. The museum is housed in the former terminal building of the city's former airport. Its interior spaces are as magnificent as its architecture, which is a remarkable example of Art Deco design. From the early 20th century to the present, the museum's collection covers more than a century of Costa Rican art, highlighting the creations of some of the most significant and influential painters in the nation.

One of the museum's most recognizable areas is the Sala de Oro (Golden Room), which has a sizable mural that shows Costa Rica's history from pre-Columbian origins until the middle of the 20th century. The mural, which was made by artist Luis Féron Parizot, is a breathtaking illustration of Costa Rican mural art and provides an eye-catching account of the nation's history. The Museo de Arte Costarricense offers a venue for fresh and avant-garde creative expressions in addition to its permanent collection via temporary exhibits that showcase the work of current artists from Costa Rica and beyond.

The Museo de Jade (Jade Museum), situated in San José, is another important Costa Rican cultural institution. The study and conservation of jade, a valuable stone that the pre-Columbian Costa Rican civilizations held in high regard, is the focus of the Museo de Jade. Thousands of jade objects, from tiny beads and amulets to huge, finely carved sculptures, are part of the museum's collection. The art and spiritual traditions of Costa Rica's ancient peoples, who thought that jade had magical and protecting qualities, are reflected in the jade pieces on show.

The museum's exhibitions provide a thorough overview of the material culture of pre-Columbian Costa Rica and include a variety of items in addition to jade, such as ceramics, stone tools, and gold objects. In order to assist visitors comprehend the importance of jade in relation to Costa Rican history and culture, the museum also provides interactive exhibits and educational activities. The Museo de Jade is a must-see for anybody with an interest in archeology, ancient art, or the history of precious stones.

Visitors may discover Costa Rica's current art scene and interact with its cultural traditions at a variety of smaller art galleries and cultural institutions in addition to these big museums. The Galería Nacional (National Gallery), housed at San José's Centro Costarricense de la Ciencia y la Cultura, is one such location. Contemporary art by well-known and up-and-coming artists from Costa Rica and other nations in the area is shown in alternating exhibits at the Galería Nacional. From painting and sculpture to photography and digital art, the gallery's shows span a broad spectrum of creative mediums and genres, making it a vibrant and captivating place for art enthusiasts.

The Centro de la Cultura Cartaginesa (Cartago Cultural Center), which is situated in Cartago, the country's former capital, is another significant cultural hub in Costa Rica. Located in a historic structure that was once a jail, the Centro de la Cultura Cartaginesa is a center for artistic and cultural endeavors in the area. The center provides a range of exhibitions and activities, such as dance workshops, music concerts, theatrical productions, and art exhibits. The Museo Municipal de Cartago, which has displays on the history and culture of Cartago, including its colonial past and its part in the fight for Costa Rican independence, is also located in the center.

The Museo Indígena Boruca (Boruca Indigenous Museum) provides a distinctive and educational experience for visitors who want to learn more about Costa Rica's indigenous traditions. The museum is devoted to conserving and disseminating the cultural legacy of the Boruca people and is situated in the southern region of the nation. Along with information on the history, language, and spiritual traditions of the Boruca people, the museum's displays include traditional Boruca masks, textiles, and ceramics. The yearly Fiesta de los Diablitos, a customary celebration honoring the Boruca's resistance to Spanish colonialism, is another event that museum visitors may learn about. To get a better knowledge of the rich cultural history of the Boruca people, the museum conducts cultural activities and guided tours.

In addition to museums and cultural institutions, Costa Rica has many outdoor cultural venues and public art projects that provide tourists with a more casual way to explore art and culture. One such area is San José's Parque Nacional, which has many monuments and sculptures that honor Costa Rica's past and culture. The park offers a serene and picturesque backdrop for taking in art and nature, and it is a well-liked meeting spot for both residents and tourists.

The Museo de Arte y Diseño Contemporáneo (Museum of Contemporary Art and Design), housed in the old National Liquor Factory in San José, is another noteworthy outdoor cultural venue. The Patio de Esculturas (Sculpture Patio), the museum's outdoor area, showcases a changing collection of modern sculptures created by Costa Rican and international artists. Additionally, the museum holds seminars, cultural events, and temporary exhibits that examine current concerns and creative approaches.

For visitors interested in learning more about Costa Rica's creative expressions and cultural legacy, the country's museums, art galleries, and cultural institutions provide a wide range of experiences. These establishments provide important insights into Costa Rica's history, identity, and inventiveness, from the pre-Columbian items at the Museo Nacional and Museo del Oro to the modern artwork at the Museo de Arte Costarricense and Galería Nacional. Regardless of your interests—archaeology, indigenous cultures, modern art, or cultural history—Costa Rica's cultural institutions are a must-see for every traveler to this stunning and culturally diverse nation.

Festivals and Events: Celebrating Costa Rican Heritage

Costa Rica is a country rich in cultural traditions, and its festivals and events are a vibrant reflection of the nation's history, values, and communal spirit. These celebrations offer visitors a unique opportunity to experience the warmth and hospitality of Costa Rican people, while also providing a deep understanding of the country's heritage. Whether you are witnessing a religious procession, participating in a lively street festival, or enjoying the rhythms of traditional music, these events are integral to the Costa Rican experience. They provide a window into the cultural fabric of the nation, making them a must-see for anyone looking to immerse themselves in the life and traditions of this beautiful country.

One of the most important celebrations in Costa Rica is Día de la Independencia (Independence Day), which is celebrated on September 15th each year. This day marks Costa Rica's independence from Spain, which was achieved in 1821. The entire country comes alive with patriotic fervor as people of all ages participate in parades, concerts, and other festivities. The day typically begins with the raising of the national flag and the singing of the national anthem, followed by a torch relay known as the Antorcha de la Libertad. The torch is passed from hand to hand, symbolizing the spread of freedom throughout the country. Schoolchildren play a central role in the celebrations, performing traditional dances, wearing colorful costumes, and marching in parades with drums and other instruments. The sense of national pride is palpable, and for visitors, it is a powerful experience to see how deeply Costa Ricans value their independence and the peace that has characterized their history.

Another major event that showcases Costa Rica's cultural heritage is the Fiestas de Palmares, held every January in the town of Palmares. This two-week-long festival is one of the largest and most anticipated events in the country, attracting hundreds of thousands of visitors. The Fiestas de Palmares are known for their vibrant mix of activities, including horse parades, bullfighting (without the killing of the bull, as Costa Rica banned this practice), concerts, and a variety of traditional foods and drinks. The festival begins with the Tope, a parade of horses and riders dressed in traditional cowboy attire, which is a nod to Costa Rica's rural heritage and the importance of cattle ranching in the country's history. Another highlight of the Fiestas de Palmares is the Carnaval, a lively street party featuring colorful floats, dancers, and musicians. The festival's atmosphere is one of joy and celebration, making it a fantastic way to experience the exuberance of Costa Rican culture.

In the month of March, Costa Rica celebrates the Día Nacional del Boyero (National Oxherd's Day), a festival dedicated to the country's traditional oxherds and their brightly painted ox carts. This event, which takes place in the town of San Antonio de Escazú, honors a practice that has been an integral part of Costa Rican rural life for centuries. The ox carts, or carretas, were once the primary means of transporting goods, particularly coffee, from the highlands to the ports. Today, the ox cart is a symbol of Costa Rican heritage, and the festival is a celebration of this cultural icon. The event includes a parade of ox carts, beautifully decorated with colorful patterns and intricate designs, drawn by pairs of oxen. The parade is accompanied by traditional music, dancing, and a blessing ceremony for the oxen. Visitors to the festival can also learn about the history of the ox cart and the craftsmanship involved in making these unique vehicles, as well as enjoy traditional foods and crafts from the region.

The Fiesta de los Diablitos (Festival of the Little Devils) is another important cultural event in Costa Rica, particularly for the Boruca indigenous community in the southern part of the country. Held annually from December 30th to January 2nd, this festival is a reenactment of the resistance of the Boruca people against Spanish colonization. The main event of the festival is a mock battle between the Diablitos (little devils), who represent the Boruca ancestors, and the Toros (bulls), symbolizing the Spanish invaders. The Diablitos wear hand-carved wooden masks, painted in vibrant colors and depicting various animals and mythical creatures. The festival is a time of cultural pride for the Boruca people, and it offers visitors a unique opportunity to witness indigenous traditions that have been passed down through generations. In addition to the reenactment, the festival includes traditional music, dance, and the sharing of chicha, a fermented corn drink that has deep cultural significance.

Another significant event that reflects Costa Rica's religious and cultural traditions is Semana Santa (Holy Week), which takes place during the week leading up to Easter. Semana Santa is observed throughout Costa Rica, with each town and city holding its own processions and religious ceremonies. The most elaborate celebrations take place in San José and Cartago, where the streets are filled with processions depicting the Passion of Christ. These processions feature participants dressed as Roman soldiers, disciples, and other biblical figures, reenacting scenes from the final days of Jesus' life. The atmosphere is solemn and reflective, with many people taking part in fasting and prayer during this time. Semana Santa is a deeply spiritual event, and for visitors, it offers an insight into the strong Catholic faith that plays a central role in the lives of many Costa Ricans. Costa Rica's Caribbean coast is home to a vibrant Afro-Caribbean community, and one of the most colorful and lively events in this region is the Carnaval de Limón. Held in October in the city of Limón, this week-long festival is a celebration of Afro-Caribbean culture, with music, dance, and food taking center stage. The Carnaval de Limón was established in the 1940s by a local community leader named Alfred Josiah Henry Smith, also known as "Mister King," who sought to bring the community together and celebrate their cultural heritage. The highlight of the festival is the Gran Desfile, a grand parade featuring elaborate costumes, floats, and dancers moving to the rhythms of calypso, reggae, and soca music. The streets of Limón come alive with the sounds of steel drums and the scent of traditional Caribbean dishes like rice and beans cooked in coconut milk, rondón (a seafood stew), and patí (a spicy meat pie). For visitors, the Carnaval de Limón is an opportunity to experience the energy and joy of Afro-Caribbean culture and to witness a different side of Costa Rica's cultural diversity.

In addition to these major festivals, Costa Rica also hosts a variety of smaller, regional events that celebrate local traditions and customs. For example, the Feria del Café (Coffee Fair) in Frailes de Desamparados, held in January, is a celebration of Costa Rica's coffee heritage. The fair features coffee tastings, tours of coffee farms, and demonstrations of traditional coffee-making techniques, as well as live music and cultural performances. The Feria de las Flores (Flower Festival) in Heredia, held in April, is another regional event that celebrates the natural beauty of Costa Rica. The festival includes a flower show, a parade of floats decorated with flowers, and a variety of cultural activities such as traditional dance performances and craft exhibitions.

The Envision Festival, held annually in Uvita on the Pacific coast, is a more contemporary event that blends music, art, and sustainability. This four-day festival attracts visitors from around the world who come to enjoy live music, workshops on topics such as yoga and permaculture, and a variety of art installations. The festival is set in a stunning natural environment, with the Pacific Ocean on one side and the rainforest on the other, making it a unique and immersive experience. The Envision Festival reflects Costa Rica's growing focus on sustainability and environmental consciousness, and it offers visitors a chance to connect with like-minded individuals and explore new ideas in a beautiful and inspiring setting.

For those interested in Costa Rica's indigenous cultures, the Feria de la Cultura Indígena (Indigenous Culture Fair) in the town of Guatuso is a significant event. Held in August, the fair brings together representatives from Costa Rica's various indigenous groups to share their traditions, crafts, and knowledge with the public. The event includes demonstrations of traditional practices such as pottery-making, weaving, and the use of medicinal plants, as well as performances of indigenous music and dance. The fair provides a platform for indigenous communities to showcase their cultural heritage and to raise awareness about the challenges they face in preserving their traditions in the modern world.

Costa Rica's festivals and events are a vibrant expression of the country's cultural heritage and offer visitors a unique opportunity to experience the richness and diversity of Costa Rican life. From the patriotic celebrations of Independence Day and the colorful parades of Carnaval de Limón to the spiritual observances of Semana Santa and the indigenous traditions of the Fiesta de los Diablitos, these events provide a deep and meaningful connection to the history, values, and communal spirit of Costa Rica. Whether you are interested in music, dance, art, or history, there is a festival or event in Costa Rica that will allow you to immerse yourself in the country's cultural landscape and to celebrate the warmth and hospitality of its people. For anyone seeking to understand Costa Rica beyond its natural beauty, participating in these festivals and events is an essential part of the experience.

Architectural Landmarks and Historical Sites

Costa Rica is a country that captivates visitors with its stunning natural landscapes and vibrant culture, but it also offers a wealth of architectural landmarks and historical sites that tell the story of its past. These sites range from colonial-era churches and forts to modernist buildings and ancient indigenous settlements, each reflecting a different aspect of the country's rich history. For tourists interested in delving deeper into Costa Rica's heritage, exploring these landmarks provides a fascinating and educational experience. These sites not only highlight the architectural styles that have shaped the country over the centuries but also serve as reminders of the social, political, and cultural forces that have influenced its development.

One of the most iconic architectural landmarks in Costa Rica is the Teatro Nacional (National Theatre), located in the heart of San José, the capital city. Built in 1897, the Teatro Nacional is a symbol of Costa Rica's cultural and artistic aspirations during the late 19th century. The building was constructed during a time of economic prosperity fueled by the coffee trade, and it reflects the influence of European architectural styles, particularly neoclassicism. The façade of the Teatro Nacional is adorned with statues representing Dance, Music, and Fame, and the interior is equally opulent, featuring marble staircases, gilded ceilings, and elaborate frescoes. The theatre's main hall is renowned for its excellent acoustics and is considered one of the most beautiful performance spaces in Central America. Visitors to the Teatro Nacional can take guided tours to learn about its history and architecture or attend one of the many performances that take place throughout the year, ranging from classical music concerts to contemporary theater productions.

Another significant historical site in Costa Rica is the Basílica de Nuestra Señora de los Ángeles (Basilica of Our Lady of the Angels) in Cartago. This church is one of the most important religious sites in the country, as it is dedicated to the patron saint of Costa Rica, the Virgen de los Ángeles.

The basilica's history dates back to the 17th century when, according to legend, a small statue of the Virgin Mary was discovered by a young girl on a rock in Cartago. The statue, known as La Negrita due to its dark color, is believed to have miraculous powers, and it quickly became a revered object of worship. The current basilica, which was completed in 1924, is a striking example of Byzantine and Romanesque architectural styles, with its grand dome, intricate stained-glass windows, and ornate altars. Each year on August 2nd, thousands of pilgrims from across Costa Rica and beyond make their way to the basilica to pay homage to La Negrita during the Romería, a pilgrimage that is one of the most significant religious events in the country.

For those interested in exploring Costa Rica's colonial history, a visit to the Ruinas de Ujarrás (Ujarrás Ruins) offers a glimpse into the country's early Spanish settlement. Located in the Orosí Valley, the Ujarrás Ruins are the remains of one of the oldest churches in Costa Rica, built in the 16th century by Spanish settlers. The church was dedicated to the Virgen del Rescate (Virgin of the Rescue), and it played a central role in the spiritual life of the early colonists. The ruins are set against a backdrop of lush green hills and offer a serene and picturesque setting for visitors to explore. Although the church was abandoned in the 19th century due to frequent flooding, the site remains a significant historical landmark, and the surrounding area is now a national monument. The Ujarrás Ruins are an evocative reminder of Costa Rica's colonial past and the challenges faced by the early settlers in this remote and rugged landscape.

Another notable historical site is the Fortín de Heredia (Heredia Fortress), located in the city of Heredia, just north of San José. The Fortín de Heredia is a small, circular tower that was built in the late 19th century as part of the city's defense system. Although it was never used in battle, the fort has become a symbol of Heredia and is one of the few remaining examples of military architecture from this period in Costa Rica. The fort's distinctive design, with its thick walls and narrow windows, reflects the military engineering of the time, and it offers a fascinating glimpse into the country's efforts to protect its towns and cities from external threats. Today, the Fortín de Heredia is a popular tourist attraction, and visitors can climb to the top of the tower for panoramic views of the city and the surrounding mountains.

In addition to its colonial and military architecture, Costa Rica is also home to a number of modernist buildings that reflect the country's growth and development in the 20th century. One such building is the Edificio Metálico (Metal Building) in San José, which is one of the city's most distinctive landmarks. The Edificio Metálico was constructed in 1892 and is made entirely of metal, including its walls, roof, and internal structure. The building was designed by the Belgian architect Charles Thirion and was manufactured in Belgium before being shipped to Costa Rica in pieces and assembled on-site. The Edificio Metálico was originally used as a school and continues to serve as an educational facility today. Its unique design and construction make it an important example of early modernist architecture in Costa Rica, and it stands as a testament to the country's embrace of new technologies and ideas during this period.

For visitors interested in pre-Columbian history, the Guayabo National Monument is an archaeological site that offers a fascinating look at one of Costa Rica's most significant ancient civilizations. Located near the town of Turrialba, Guayabo is believed to have been inhabited from around 1000 BCE to 1400 CE, and it was one of the largest and most important settlements in pre-Columbian Costa Rica. The site covers an area of over 200 hectares, although only a small portion has been excavated. Visitors to Guayabo can explore the remains of ancient stone structures, including roads, aqueducts, plazas, and tombs, as well as a ceremonial center with a large stone platform. The site's advanced engineering, particularly its water management systems, reflects the sophistication of the society that built it. Guayabo is a UNESCO World Heritage site and is considered one of the most important archaeological sites in Central America. A visit to Guayabo offers a rare opportunity to connect with the ancient history of Costa Rica and to appreciate the achievements of its early inhabitants.

Another significant archaeological site is the Stone Spheres of the Diquís, located in the Diquís Delta in the southern part of Costa Rica. These enigmatic stone spheres, known locally as Las Bolas, were created by the pre-Columbian Diquís culture and are believed to date back to between 300 BCE and 1500 CE. The spheres vary in size, with some measuring over two meters in diameter and weighing several tons. The purpose of the spheres remains a mystery, although it is believed that they may have been used for ceremonial or astronomical purposes. The Stone Spheres of the Diquís are remarkable for their near-perfect roundness and the skill required to carve them from solid stone using only rudimentary tools. In 2014, the spheres were designated as a UNESCO World Heritage site, and they continue to be a subject of fascination for archaeologists and visitors alike.

In the city of Alajuela, the Juan Santamaría Historical Museum offers visitors an in-depth look at one of Costa Rica's most celebrated national heroes. Juan Santamaría was a young drummer boy who played a key role in the Battle of Rivas in 1856, during Costa Rica's conflict with the American filibuster William Walker. Santamaría's bravery in setting fire to the enemy stronghold, at the cost of his own life, has made him a symbol of national pride and resistance. The museum, located in a historic building that was once a military barracks, houses exhibit on the life and legacy of Juan Santamaría, as well as the broader history of Costa Rica during this tumultuous period. The museum's collections include military artifacts, documents, and artworks that provide a comprehensive overview of the events that shaped Costa Rica's national identity. Visitors to the Juan Santamaría Historical Museum can gain a deeper understanding of the country's struggle for sovereignty and the enduring legacy of its national hero.

Another important cultural site in Costa Rica is the Museo Histórico Cultural Juan Santamaría (Juan Santamaría Historical and Cultural Museum) in Alajuela. This museum is dedicated to the history and culture of Costa Rica, with a particular focus on the 19th century and the events surrounding the country's fight for independence and sovereignty. The museum is housed in a former military barracks and features exhibits on topics such as the Battle of Rivas, the legacy of Juan Santamaría, and the social and political changes that took place in Costa Rica during the 19th century. The museum's collections include historical artifacts, documents, and artworks that provide a comprehensive overview of Costa Rica's history and culture. The Museo Histórico Cultural Juan Santamaría is an important resource for anyone interested in learning more about the country's past and the forces that have shaped its present.

Costa Rica's architectural landmarks and historical sites offer a rich and varied exploration of the country's history, culture, and identity. From the neoclassical elegance of the Teatro Nacional to the ancient stone spheres of the Diquís, these sites provide a window into the past and a deeper understanding of the forces that have shaped Costa Rica into the nation it is today. Whether you are exploring the ruins of colonial-era churches, marveling at the engineering achievements of ancient civilizations, or learning about the country's national heroes, these landmarks offer a valuable and educational experience for anyone interested in delving into the history and heritage of Costa Rica. For tourists seeking to go beyond the natural beauty of the country and connect with its cultural roots, visiting these sites is an essential part of the journey.

CHAPTER 10

SHOPPING AND SOUVENIRS

Markets and Artisan Crafts

Costa Rica is a country known for its breathtaking landscapes, abundant wildlife, and warm-hearted people, but one of the most authentic ways to experience its culture is through its vibrant markets and exquisite artisan crafts. These markets are more than just places to buy goods; they are dynamic social hubs where locals and visitors alike can connect, share stories, and immerse themselves in the rich traditions that define Costa Rican life. For tourists, exploring these markets and discovering the handcrafted treasures within offers a deeper understanding of the country's cultural heritage and a unique way to bring a piece of Costa Rica home.

The markets in Costa Rica are diverse, ranging from bustling urban markets filled with fresh produce and everyday necessities to small, specialized artisan markets where craftsmanship and creativity take center stage. Each market reflects the unique character of the region it serves, and together, they offer a comprehensive picture of the country's rich cultural tapestry.

One of the most famous markets in Costa Rica is the Mercado Central (Central Market) in San José, the capital city. Established in 1880, Mercado Central is a labyrinth of narrow aisles and vibrant stalls that is both chaotic and charming. The market is a sensory feast, with the aromas of fresh coffee, spices, and cooked food mingling in the air, and the vibrant colors of tropical fruits, vegetables, and artisan goods providing a visual treat. Mercado Central is a place where locals come to shop for their daily needs, and it offers tourists an authentic glimpse into everyday Costa Rican life. Visitors can find everything from fresh produce and meats to traditional Costa Rican dishes like gallo pinto (rice and beans) and casado (a typical lunch plate), as well as a variety of artisan crafts.

Within Mercado Central, you will also find stalls selling souvernirs and handicrafts, including some of the most iconic Costa Rican items such as oxcart miniatures and hand-painted ceramics. The ox cart, or carreta, is a symbol of Costa Rican culture and history. Originally used to transport coffee beans from the Central Valley to the coastal ports, these carts are now celebrated for their bright, intricate designs, which often feature geometric patterns and vibrant colors. Artisans who specialize in oxcart painting apply their skills to a variety of products, creating beautiful and functional items that are deeply rooted in Costa Rican tradition. A miniature oxcart makes for a perfect souvenir, embodying the craftsmanship and cultural significance of this national symbol.

Another popular destination for artisan crafts in San José is the Feria Verde de Aranjuez, a weekly market that focuses on organic products, sustainability, and local craftsmanship. Held every Saturday morning, this market is a favorite among locals and expatriates who value healthy living and environmental consciousness. The Feria Verde is not just a place to buy organic fruits and vegetables; it's also a hub for local artisans who produce handmade goods such as jewelry, clothing, and natural beauty products. The market has a relaxed, community-oriented atmosphere, making it an ideal spot for tourists to mingle with locals and discover unique, high-quality crafts that are made with care and respect for the environment.

Outside of San José, many other regions of Costa Rica have their own distinctive markets and artisan traditions. In the town of Sarchí, located in the province of Alajuela, visitors will find one of the most renowned centers for traditional woodworking and craftmanship in the country. Sarchí is famously known as the birthplace of the painted oxcart, and the town is filled with workshops where skilled artisans continue this time-honored craft. The attention to detail and the vibrant use of color in Sarchí's oxcarts are truly remarkable, and visitors can watch artisans at work, creating not only oxcarts but also a wide range of wooden furniture and decorative items. These workshops often double as showrooms, where visitors can purchase beautifully crafted pieces that reflect the artistic heritage of the region.

Sarchí is also home to the Iglesia de Sarchí, a picturesque church that features elements of the local artisan style. The church's vibrant façade, painted in the same bright colors and patterns as the oxcarts, is a testament to the town's pride in its artisan heritage. Visiting Sarchí provides a unique opportunity to see the close connection between the local culture, craftsmanship, and community identity.

In the northwestern region of Costa Rica, the province of Guanacaste is famous for its pottery, which has been produced by the indigenous Chorotega people for centuries. The town of Guaitil is the epicenter of this ancient craft, and it is here that visitors can witness the traditional methods of pottery-making that have been passed down through generations. The clay used in Guaitil pottery is sourced locally, and artisans use techniques that have changed little over the centuries, such as hand-coiling and burnishing. The pottery is often adorned with intricate geometric patterns and natural motifs, which are painted using mineral-based pigments. These designs are not only aesthetically pleasing but also hold cultural significance, reflecting the Chorotega's connection to the land and their ancestors. Visitors to Guaitil can purchase pottery directly from the artisans, ensuring that their purchases support the continuation of this important cultural tradition.

The town of Nicoya, also located in Guanacaste, is another important center for artisan crafts. Nicoya is known for its vibrant celebrations of traditional festivals, during which the town comes alive with music, dance, and artisan markets. The crafts available in Nicoya include traditional clothing, handwoven baskets, and other items that are integral to the cultural identity of the region. The town's markets are especially lively during the Fiestas de Nicoya, which are held in honor of the patron saint, San Blas. During this time, visitors can experience the full richness of Guanacaste's artisan traditions and take home unique, handcrafted items that are steeped in local history.

Another important artisan tradition in Costa Rica is mask-making, which is particularly associated with the indigenous Boruca people. The Boruca are known for their Diablitos masks, which are used in the annual Fiesta de los Diablitos. These masks are intricately carved from balsa wood and painted in vibrant colors, often featuring animal or mythological designs. The masks are not only artistic creations but also hold deep cultural and spiritual significance for the Boruca people, symbolizing their resistance to Spanish colonization and their connection to the natural world. Visitors to Boruca communities can purchase these masks directly from the artisans, and they can also learn about the cultural importance of the masks through demonstrations and storytelling.

For tourists interested in exploring the markets and artisan crafts of Costa Rica, it's important to approach these experiences with respect and an appreciation for the cultural significance of the items being purchased. Many of the artisans who produce these crafts rely on their work as a primary source of income, and purchasing directly from them helps to support their livelihoods and the preservation of traditional practices. Additionally, buying artisan crafts in Costa Rica provides an opportunity to bring home meaningful souvenirs that reflect the country's rich cultural heritage.

The markets and artisan crafts of Costa Rica offer a fascinating and authentic glimpse into the country's cultural landscape. From the bustling stalls of Mercado Central in San José to the artisan workshops of Sarchí and the pottery studios of Guaitil, these places are where tradition and creativity come together to produce beautiful, handcrafted items that are deeply connected to Costa Rican identity. For tourists, exploring these markets is not just about shopping; it's about engaging with the culture, learning about the history and significance of these crafts, and supporting the artisans who keep these traditions alive. Whether you're purchasing a hand-painted oxcart, a piece of Chorotega pottery, or a Boruca mask, these items are more than just souvenirs—they are tangible connections to the heart and soul of Costa Rica.

Best Places to Buy Coffee and Chocolate

Costa Rica is a country renowned for its rich natural resources, and two of its most celebrated exports are coffee and chocolate. These products are not just commodities; they are deeply intertwined with the country's history, culture, and economy. For tourists visiting Costa Rica, exploring the best places to buy coffee and chocolate is an experience that goes beyond mere shopping. It's an opportunity to engage with the local traditions, learn about the processes behind these beloved products, and take home a piece of Costa Rican culture. Whether you are a connoisseur or simply a curious traveler, the journey to find the finest coffee and chocolate in Costa Rica is one that is sure to be both educational and delightful.

Costa Rican coffee is often considered some of the best in the world, and its reputation is well-deserved. The country's unique climate, with its high altitudes, rich volcanic soil, and ideal temperatures, creates the perfect conditions for growing coffee. Coffee production in Costa Rica dates back to the early 19th century, and it quickly became one of the country's most important industries. Today, coffee remains a key export, and the tradition of coffee cultivation is a source of national pride. For tourists looking to purchase the best coffee in Costa Rica, there are several regions and specific locations that are known for producing exceptional beans.

One of the most famous coffee-growing regions in Costa Rica is the Central Valley, which is home to some of the country's oldest and most prestigious coffee plantations. The Central Valley's elevation, fertile soil, and mild climate make it an ideal location for coffee cultivation, and the beans produced here are known for their balanced flavor, with notes of fruit, chocolate, and nuts. In the Central Valley, one of the best places to buy coffee is Café Britt, a well-known brand that has been producing high-quality coffee for decades. Café Britt offers a wide range of coffee products, from single-origin beans to specialty blends, and they also provide tours of their coffee plantation and roastery, where visitors can learn about the entire process, from the planting of the coffee trees to the roasting of the beans. The tour includes a tasting session, allowing visitors to sample different types of coffee and discover their preferred flavor profiles. At the end of the tour, visitors can purchase freshly roasted coffee beans, ensuring that they take home a truly authentic Costa Rican coffee experience.

Another excellent destination for coffee lovers is the Tarrazú region, located south of San José. Tarrazú is often referred to as the "Bordeaux of coffee," due to the exceptional quality of the beans produced in this region. The coffee from Tarrazú is known for its bright acidity, full body, and complex flavor profile, with hints of citrus and tropical fruit. One of the best places to buy coffee in Tarrazú is from the Cooperativa de Caficultores de Tarrazú (COOPETARRAZÚ), a cooperative that represents hundreds of small coffee growers in the region. The cooperative offers a variety of coffee products, including single-origin beans and specialty blends, and they are committed to sustainable and ethical farming practices. Visitors to Tarrazú can tour the cooperative's facilities, learn about the coffee production process, and purchase freshly roasted beans directly from the source.

For those interested in organic and sustainable coffee, the Monteverde region is a must-visit. Monteverde, located in the cloud forests of the Puntarenas province, is known for its commitment to environmental conservation, and this ethos extends to its coffee production. The coffee produced in Monteverde is often grown on small, family-owned farms that prioritize organic and sustainable farming practices. One of the best places to buy coffee in Monteverde is from the Café de Monteverde cooperative, which produces organic, shade-grown coffee. The cooperative offers tours of their coffee farm, where visitors can learn about the benefits of shade-grown coffee, which not only produces high-quality beans but also helps to preserve the biodiversity of the cloud forest. After the tour, visitors can purchase freshly roasted coffee beans, which are available in a variety of roasts and flavor profiles.

In addition to coffee, Costa Rica is also known for its high-quality chocolate, which has a long history in the country. Cacao, the primary ingredient in chocolate, has been cultivated in Central America for thousands of years, and it was used by indigenous peoples for both culinary and ceremonial purposes. Today, Costa Rica is experiencing a renaissance in chocolate production, with many small-scale producers focusing on artisanal and organic chocolate that highlights the unique flavors of Costa Rican cacao.

One of the best places to buy chocolate in Costa Rica is the Caribbean coast, particularly in the province of Limón. This region has a long history of cacao cultivation, and it is home to some of the country's finest chocolate producers. One of the most well-known chocolate makers in the region is Caribeans Coffee & Chocolate, located in Puerto Viejo. Caribeans is a small, family-owned business that produces organic, bean-to-bar chocolate using locally sourced cacao. Visitors to Caribeans can tour their chocolate farm and factory, where they can learn about the entire chocolate-making process, from the harvesting of the cacao pods to the crafting of the finished chocolate bars. The tour includes a tasting session, allowing visitors to sample a variety of chocolate products, each with its own unique flavor profile. Caribeans offers a range of chocolate bars, including single-origin and flavored varieties, and their products are available for purchase at their shop in Puerto Viejo.

Another excellent destination for chocolate lovers is the Talamanca region, which is home to several indigenous communities that have been growing and using cacao for centuries. One of the best places to buy chocolate in Talamanca is from the Bribri people, who produce chocolate using traditional methods passed down through generations. The Bribri use cacao in a variety of ways, including making a traditional drink called cacaoti, which is made by grinding roasted cacao beans and mixing them with water and spices. Visitors to the Bribri communities can learn about the cultural significance of cacao, participate in a chocolate-making workshop, and purchase handmade chocolate products directly from the artisans. These chocolates are often made using minimal ingredients, allowing the rich flavor of the cacao to shine through.

In the Central Valley, the town of Sarchí is not only known for its artisan crafts but also for its high-quality chocolate. Sibu Chocolate, located near Sarchí, is one of the country's premier chocolate makers, producing gourmet chocolate using organic, locally sourced cacao. Sibu is known for its commitment to sustainability and fair trade, and they work closely with small-scale cacao farmers to ensure that their chocolate is both ethically produced and of the highest quality. Visitors to Sibu can tour their chocolate workshop, where they can learn about the art of chocolate-making and sample a variety of chocolate products. Sibu offers a wide range of chocolate bars, truffles, and other confections, each carefully crafted to highlight the unique flavors of Costa Rican cacao.

For those looking to explore the fusion of coffee and chocolate, Café Britt offers a range of products that combine the two, including chocolate-covered coffee beans and gourmet hot chocolate mixes. These products make for excellent gifts and souvenirs, as they capture the essence of Costa Rica's rich agricultural heritage.

Costa Rica offers a wealth of opportunities for tourists to explore and purchase some of the world's finest coffee and chocolate. From the lush coffee plantations of the Central Valley and Tarrazú to the cacao-rich regions of the Caribbean coast and Talamanca, the country's diverse landscapes produce a wide range of flavors and products that reflect the rich cultural and agricultural traditions of Costa Rica. Whether you are a coffee aficionado or a chocolate lover, visiting these regions and purchasing products directly from the producers not only ensures that you take home high-quality goods but also supports the local communities and helps to preserve these important traditions. The journey to find the best coffee and chocolate in Costa Rica is one that is sure to be both educational and deeply satisfying, offering a true taste of the country's rich heritage.

CHAPTER 12

ITINERARIES FOR EVERY TRAVELER

7-Day Itinerary for First-Time Visitors

Costa Rica is a country that offers a perfect blend of natural beauty, adventure, and cultural experiences. For first-time visitors, planning a 7-day itinerary that allows you to experience the best of what Costa Rica has to offer can be both exciting and overwhelming.

Day 1: Arrival in San José

Your adventure begins in San José, the capital of Costa Rica. San José is often seen as a gateway to the rest of the country, but it's worth spending a day exploring the city's cultural and historical sites. Upon arrival, take some time to relax and acclimate to the warm climate. If you arrive early enough, you can start your exploration right away.

A great starting point is the Teatro Nacional (National Theatre), an architectural masterpiece located in the heart of the city. This iconic building, constructed in the late 19th century, is a symbol of Costa Rica's cultural heritage. Take a guided tour to appreciate its neoclassical architecture, ornate interiors, and the famous mural "Alegoría del Café y el Banano" (Allegory of Coffee and Bananas).

After visiting the theatre, head to the nearby Museo del Oro Precolombino (Pre-Columbian Gold Museum), which houses an impressive collection of pre-Columbian gold artifacts. This museum offers a fascinating glimpse into the lives and customs of the indigenous peoples who inhabited the region long before the arrival of Europeans.

In the evening, explore the bustling Barrio Amón or Barrio Escalante neighborhoods, known for their vibrant nightlife, restaurants, and bars. This is the perfect opportunity to sample some local cuisine. Try traditional dishes like casado (a hearty plate of rice, beans, meat, and plantains) or gallo pinto (a classic breakfast dish of rice and beans) at one of the many local eateries.

Day 2: Journey to Arenal Volcano

On your second day, leave San José behind and head to the Arenal Volcano region, one of Costa Rica's most iconic destinations. The drive to Arenal takes about three hours, and along the way, you'll be treated to scenic views of lush valleys, mountains, and quaint villages.

Once you arrive in the town of La Fortuna, which is situated at the base of the Arenal Volcano, you'll immediately notice the dramatic landscape dominated by the towering, symmetrical cone of the volcano. Arenal is an active volcano, but it has been in a resting phase since 2010, making it safe for visitors to explore the surrounding area.

Begin your exploration with a visit to the Arenal Volcano National Park. The park offers a variety of trails that wind through lush forests, past lava fields, and up to viewpoints that offer stunning vistas of the volcano and the surrounding countryside. The Las Coladas trail is a popular choice, taking you across old lava flows from past eruptions.

After a day of hiking, reward yourself with a visit to one of the many hot springs in the area. The hot springs are naturally heated by the geothermal activity of the volcano and offer a relaxing way to unwind. Tabacón Hot Springs is one of the most famous and luxurious options, but there are also more budget-friendly choices like Eco Termales or Baldi Hot Springs.

Day 3: Adventure in Arenal

Arenal is a hub for outdoor activities and adventure, making it the perfect place to spend a day full of excitement. Start your day with a thrilling zip-lining tour that takes you high above the treetops. As you soar through the canopy, you'll have a bird's-eye view of the lush forest below, and on a clear day, you might even catch a glimpse of the Arenal Volcano in the distance.

After the adrenaline rush of zip-lining, slow things down with a visit to La Fortuna Waterfall. The waterfall is located just a short drive from La Fortuna, and a well-maintained trail leads you down to the base of the falls. The powerful cascade plunges 70 meters into a clear pool, surrounded by dense jungle. You can take a refreshing swim in the cool waters or simply relax and enjoy the natural beauty of the area.

In the afternoon, embark on a hanging bridges tour in the Mistico Arenal Hanging Bridges Park. This series of suspension bridges and well-maintained trails takes you through the rainforest canopy, offering a unique perspective on the flora and fauna of the region. Keep your eyes peeled for wildlife such as monkeys, sloths, and a variety of bird species.

As the day comes to an end, head back to La Fortuna for a leisurely evening. Enjoy a dinner at one of the town's many restaurants, where you can savor local specialties like ceviche or grilled meats.

Day 4: Monteverde Cloud Forest

On day four, it's time to leave the volcanic landscapes of Arenal and make your way to the mystical cloud forests of Monteverde. The drive to Monteverde takes about three to four hours and includes some bumpy roads, but the journey is well worth it. The change in scenery is dramatic as you ascend into the cool, misty heights of the cloud forest.

Monteverde is famous for its unique cloud forest ecosystem, where the high altitude and constant mist create a lush, verdant environment teeming with biodiversity. Upon arrival, visit the Monteverde Cloud Forest Reserve, one of the most renowned cloud forests in the world. The reserve is home to a staggering variety of plants, animals, and birds, including the elusive resplendent quetzal.

Take a guided hike through the reserve, where you'll learn about the delicate balance of this ecosystem and the efforts to conserve it. The trails are well-marked and range from easy to moderate, making them accessible to most visitors. The Sendero Bosque Nuboso (Cloud Forest Trail) is a popular option, offering a good mix of scenery and wildlife spotting opportunities.

After your hike, visit the Monteverde Butterfly Garden or the Bat Jungle for a closer look at some of the smaller inhabitants of the cloud forest. In the evening, consider joining a night walk tour, where you can experience the forest after dark and encounter nocturnal creatures such as frogs, insects, and possibly even a kinkajou.

Day 5: Explore Monteverde

Monteverde is a place where you can easily spend an entire day exploring its natural wonders and engaging in eco-friendly activities. Start your day with a visit to the Santa Elena Cloud Forest Reserve, another beautiful reserve in the area. While similar to the Monteverde Cloud Forest Reserve, Santa Elena is slightly higher in elevation and tends to be less crowded, offering a more tranquil experience. The trails here are well-maintained, and the reserve is a great place to spot birds, including hummingbirds and trogons.

For a more adventurous experience, consider a canopy tour that combines zip-lining with a series of hanging bridges.

This will give you a different perspective of the cloud forest as you move from tree to tree, high above the forest floor.

In the afternoon, visit a local coffee plantation to learn about one of Costa Rica's most important exports. The Don Juan Coffee Tour or the El Trapiche Tour are excellent options, offering insights into the coffee-making process from bean to cup. You'll also have the opportunity to taste freshly brewed coffee and purchase some to take home as a souvenir.

For dinner, try one of Monteverde's farm-to-table restaurants, where you can enjoy dishes made with fresh, locally sourced ingredients. Monteverde is known for its commitment to sustainability, and many of the town's restaurants reflect this ethos.

Day 6: Travel to Manuel Antonio

On day six, it's time to leave the cool cloud forests behind and head to the warm, sun-soaked beaches of Manuel Antonio on the Pacific coast. The drive to Manuel Antonio takes about four to five hours, but the journey offers beautiful views as you descend from the mountains to the coast.

Manuel Antonio is one of Costa Rica's most popular beach destinations, and for good reason. The area is home to Manuel Antonio National Park, a small but biodiverse park that combines lush rainforest with stunning beaches. After checking into your accommodation, spend the afternoon exploring the park's trails and beaches.

The park's main trail leads to several picturesque beaches, including Playa Manuel Antonio, which is often considered one of the most beautiful beaches in Costa Rica. The clear, turquoise waters are perfect for swimming, snorkeling, or simply relaxing on the sand. As you explore the park, keep an eye out for wildlife such as sloths, monkeys, and colorful birds.

In the evening, take a stroll along Playa Espadilla, a long stretch of beach just outside the park, where you can watch the sunset over the Pacific Ocean. There are plenty of beachfront restaurants where you can enjoy fresh seafood and tropical cocktails while taking in the views.

Day 7: Relax and Explore Manuel Antonio

Your final day in Costa Rica is all about relaxation and enjoying the natural beauty of Manuel Antonio. Start your day with a leisurely breakfast, and then head back to Manuel Antonio National Park for more exploration. You might choose to revisit one of the beaches, take another hike, or simply enjoy the peaceful surroundings.

If you're looking for more adventure, consider taking a kayaking tour through the nearby mangroves or going on a catamaran cruise, which often includes snorkeling and the chance to see dolphins and other marine life.

For those who prefer to stay on land, horseback riding tours are available, offering a unique way to explore the surrounding countryside. You can ride through the forest, along the beach, or to a nearby waterfall, all while enjoying the natural beauty of the area.

As the day winds down, take some time to reflect on your journey through Costa Rica. Whether you choose to spend your final evening enjoying a quiet dinner or watching the sunset from a beachside bar, you'll leave with memories of a diverse and enchanting country that has something to offer every traveler.

Departure

On the eighth day, it's time to say goodbye to Costa Rica. Depending on your departure time, you might have a few hours to relax on the beach or do some last-minute shopping for souvenirs before heading to the airport in San José.

Costa Rica is a destination that captures the hearts of those who visit. From its active volcanoes and misty cloud forests to its stunning beaches and rich biodiversity, this 7-day itinerary provides a taste of the many wonders that make Costa Rica such a beloved destination. For first-time visitors, this journey offers a well-rounded introduction to the country, leaving you with a deep appreciation for its natural beauty, cultural richness, and the warm hospitality of its people. Whether you're seeking adventure, relaxation, or cultural experiences, Costa Rica has something to offer, making it a destination you'll want to return to again and again.

10-Day Itinerary for Adventure Seekers

Costa Rica is a paradise for adventure seekers, offering an unparalleled mix of natural beauty, diverse ecosystems, and thrilling activities. For those who crave excitement and want to immerse themselves in the wild heart of this Central American country, a 10-day itinerary can provide the perfect balance of adrenaline-pumping experiences and opportunities to connect with nature. This journey will take you from the rugged mountains and volcanoes to the dense rainforests and pristine coastlines, offering a comprehensive and exhilarating exploration of what Costa Rica has to offer.

Day 1: Arrival in San José and Transfer to Tortuguero

Your adventure begins in San José, the capital of Costa Rica. After landing at Juan Santamaría International Airport, you'll embark on your first journey to the remote and wild Tortuguero National Park, located on the Caribbean coast. The journey to Tortuguero is part of the adventure itself, as it involves a combination of a scenic drive through the Braulio Carrillo National Park followed by a boat ride through the lush canals of Tortuguero. The boat ride offers your first glimpse of the rich biodiversity that Costa Rica is famous for, with the chance to spot birds, monkeys, and caimans along the way.

Once you arrive in Tortuguero, you'll check into your lodge, which will likely be surrounded by the dense rainforest. Spend the rest of the day exploring the nearby village of Tortuguero or relaxing at your lodge. The sound of the jungle will be your constant companion, setting the tone for the adventures that lie ahead.

Day 2: Exploring Tortuguero National Park

Tortuguero National Park is a haven for wildlife and offers some of the best opportunities for adventure and exploration. Begin your day with an early morning boat tour through the park's extensive network of canals. These waterways are the lifeblood of the park and are teeming with life. As you glide through the calm waters, you'll have the chance to spot a variety of animals, including howler monkeys, sloths, toucans, and, if you're lucky, manatees. The early morning hours are the best time to observe wildlife, as the animals are most active during this time.

After your boat tour, you can explore the park further by taking a guided hike through the jungle. The trails in Tortuguero offer an immersive experience in one of the most biodiverse regions of Costa Rica. Your guide will point out various plants and animals, and you'll learn about the complex ecosystems that make Tortuguero so unique.

In the afternoon, take some time to relax on the beach. Tortuguero is famous for being one of the most important nesting sites for sea turtles in the world. Depending on the time of year (from July to October), you might be able to join a guided night tour to witness the incredible spectacle of sea turtles laying their eggs on the beach.

Day 3: Whitewater Rafting on the Pacuare River

On the third day, your adventure takes you to the Pacuare River, widely regarded as one of the best whitewater rafting rivers in the world. The Pacuare River winds through dense jungle, steep canyons, and stunning waterfalls, offering both challenging rapids and breathtaking scenery. The day begins with an early morning transfer to the river, where you'll meet your rafting guides and receive a safety briefing.

The rafting adventure on the Pacuare River is an exhilarating experience, with rapids ranging from class III to class IV. As you navigate the river's twists and turns, you'll be surrounded by towering cliffs, cascading waterfalls, and lush rainforest. Along the way, there will be opportunities to stop and explore the riverbanks, where you can take a swim in natural pools or hike to hidden waterfalls.

The rafting trip includes a riverside lunch, giving you a chance to recharge before tackling the next set of rapids. By the end of the day, you'll have covered a significant portion of the river, and your adventure will conclude at a remote jungle lodge where you can relax and recount the day's excitement.

Day 4: Transfer to Arenal Volcano and Hot Springs

After your thrilling rafting adventure, it's time to head to the Arenal Volcano region, one of Costa Rica's most iconic destinations. The transfer to Arenal takes you through the scenic countryside, with views of rolling hills, coffee plantations, and small villages.

Upon arriving in the town of La Fortuna, you'll immediately notice the imposing presence of Arenal Volcano, a nearly perfect conical volcano that dominates the landscape. Although Arenal has been in a resting phase since 2010, it remains one of the most recognizable and photographed landmarks in Costa Rica.

After checking into your accommodation, spend the afternoon exploring the area or relaxing in one of the many hot springs that are naturally heated by the geothermal activity of the volcano. The hot springs are the perfect way to unwind after a day of travel and adventure, with pools of varying temperatures set in lush, tropical gardens. Tabacón Hot Springs is one of the most luxurious options, but there are also more budget-friendly choices like Baldi Hot Springs or Eco Termales.

Day 5: Canyoning and Waterfall Rappelling in Arenal

Your fifth day in Costa Rica is all about adventure and pushing your limits with a canyoning and waterfall rappelling experience in the Arenal region. Canyoning, also known as canyoneering, involves navigating through a canyon by rappelling down waterfalls, jumping into pools, and climbing over rocks. It's an activity that combines adrenaline with the beauty of nature, making it perfect for adventure seekers.

The day begins with a transfer to the canyoning site, where you'll meet your guides and receive a safety briefing. After gearing up, you'll start your descent into the canyon, rappelling down a series of waterfalls ranging from 20 to 200 feet in height. The experience is exhilarating, as you lower yourself down the waterfalls, feeling the cool water cascading over you. In between rappels, there are opportunities to swim in natural pools and hike through the jungle.

Canyoning in the Arenal region offers a unique way to experience the area's natural beauty, with stunning views of the surrounding rainforest and the Arenal Volcano in the distance. After a day of adventure, return to your accommodation in La Fortuna and relax for the evening.

Day 6: Zip-Lining and Hanging Bridges in Monteverde

On day six, you'll leave the Arenal region and head to the misty cloud forests of Monteverde, a place known for its unique ecosystems and adventure activities. The journey to Monteverde takes you around Lake Arenal and through mountainous terrain, with breathtaking views along the way.

Monteverde is famous for its cloud forests, where the high altitude and constant mist create a lush, verdant environment teeming with biodiversity. The first activity on your agenda is a zip-lining tour, one of the most popular adventures in Monteverde. The zip-lining courses in Monteverde are some of the best in Costa Rica, offering long, high-speed rides through the treetops with spectacular views of the forest below. The adrenaline rush of flying through the air, combined with the beauty of the cloud forest, makes this an unforgettable experience.

After zip-lining, explore the forest from a different perspective with a visit to the Monteverde Hanging Bridges. These suspension bridges are part of a network of trails that take you through the forest canopy, offering a chance to observe the flora and fauna up close. The hanging bridges are a great way to experience the cloud forest's unique ecosystem, with opportunities to see birds, monkeys, and other wildlife.

In the evening, consider joining a night walk tour to experience the cloud forest after dark. The forest comes alive at night, with nocturnal creatures such as frogs, insects, and possibly even a kinkajou making appearances.

Day 7: Exploring Monteverde's Cloud Forests

Monteverde offers endless opportunities for adventure and exploration, and day seven is dedicated to immersing yourself in the natural wonders of the cloud forests. Begin your day with a visit to the Monteverde Cloud Forest Reserve, one of the most renowned cloud forests in the world. The reserve is home to a staggering variety of plants, animals, and birds, including the elusive resplendent quetzal.
Take a guided hike through the reserve, where you'll learn about the delicate balance of this ecosystem and the efforts to conserve it. The trails are well-marked and range from easy to moderate, making them accessible to most visitors. The Sendero Bosque Nuboso (Cloud Forest Trail) is a popular

option, offering a good mix of scenery and wildlife spotting opportunities.

After your hike, visit the Santa Elena Cloud Forest Reserve, another beautiful reserve in the area. While similar to the Monteverde Cloud Forest Reserve, Santa Elena is slightly higher in elevation and tends to be less crowded, offering a more tranquil experience. The trails here are well-maintained, and the reserve is a great place to spot birds, including hummingbirds and trogons.

For a more adventurous experience, consider a canopy tour that combines zip-lining with a series of hanging bridges. This will give you a different perspective of the cloud forest as you move from tree to tree, high above the forest floor.

Day 8: Travel to Manuel Antonio

On day eight, it's time to leave the cool cloud forests behind and head to the warm, sun-soaked beaches of Manuel Antonio on the Pacific coast. The drive to Manuel Antonio takes about four to five hours, but the journey offers beautiful views as you descend from the mountains to the coast.

Manuel Antonio is one of Costa Rica's most popular beach destinations, and for good reason. The area is home to Manuel Antonio National Park, a small but biodiverse park that combines lush rainforest with stunning beaches. After checking into your accommodation, spend the afternoon exploring the park's trails and beaches.

The park's main trail leads to several picturesque beaches, including Playa Manuel Antonio, which is often considered one of the most beautiful beaches in Costa Rica. The clear, turquoise waters are perfect for swimming, snorkeling, or simply relaxing on the sand. As you explore the park, keep an eye out for wildlife such as sloths, monkeys, and colorful birds.

In the evening, take a stroll along Playa Espadilla, a long stretch of beach just outside the park, where you can watch the sunset over the Pacific Ocean. There are plenty of beachfront restaurants where you can enjoy fresh seafood and tropical cocktails while taking in the views.

Day 9: Surfing and Adventure in Manuel Antonio

Manuel Antonio is a paradise for adventure seekers, offering a variety of activities that take advantage of the area's natural beauty. Start your day with a surfing lesson on Playa Espadilla, one of the best beaches for beginners. The gentle waves and warm waters make it an ideal spot to learn how to surf, and there are plenty of surf schools and instructors available to help you get started.

After your surfing session, consider taking a kayaking tour through the nearby mangroves or going on a catamaran cruise, which often includes snorkeling and the chance to see dolphins and other marine life.

For those who prefer to stay on land, horseback riding tours are available, offering a unique way to explore the surrounding countryside. You can ride through the forest, along the beach, or to a nearby waterfall, all while enjoying the natural beauty of the area.

As the day winds down, take some time to reflect on your journey through Costa Rica. Whether you choose to spend your final evening enjoying a quiet dinner or watching the sunset from a beachside bar, you'll leave with memories of a diverse and enchanting country that has something to offer every traveler.

Day 10: Departure

On the final day of your adventure-filled itinerary, you'll return to San José for your departure. Depending on your flight time, you may have some extra hours in the morning to enjoy the beach or do some last-minute shopping for souvenirs. As you leave Costa Rica, you'll carry with you the memories of an incredible journey, filled with adrenaline, awe-inspiring landscapes, and unforgettable experiences.

This 10-day itinerary for adventure seekers in Costa Rica offers a comprehensive and thrilling exploration of the country's diverse natural beauty and exhilarating activities. From the wild canals of Tortuguero and the roaring rapids of the Pacuare River to the majestic Arenal Volcano, the misty cloud forests of Monteverde, and the sun-kissed beaches of Manuel Antonio, this journey is designed to satisfy your thirst for adventure and leave you with a deep appreciation for the rich and varied landscapes of Costa Rica.

14-Day Itinerary for Families

Planning a 14-day family vacation in Costa Rica is an excellent way to explore the country's diverse landscapes, wildlife, and cultural experiences while ensuring that every member of the family has an unforgettable time. Costa Rica is a perfect destination for families because it offers a wide range of activities that cater to different ages and interests, from exploring rainforests and volcanoes to relaxing on beautiful beaches. This detailed itinerary is designed to give families a comprehensive and enjoyable experience, allowing them to connect with nature, learn about Costa Rican culture, and have fun together in a safe and welcoming environment.

Day 1: Arrival in San José

Your family adventure begins in San José, the capital of Costa Rica. After arriving at Juan Santamaría International Airport, take some time to settle into your accommodation and adjust to the warm climate. Depending on your arrival time, you can start exploring the city or simply relax and recover from your flight.

If you have some energy left, a visit to the Parque La Sabana is a great way to stretch your legs. This large urban park is perfect for families, offering plenty of green space, playgrounds, and a lake where you can rent paddleboats. It's a nice introduction to Costa Rica's outdoor lifestyle, and the kids will appreciate the chance to run around and play.

For dinner, consider visiting one of the local restaurants in the Barrio Escalante neighborhood, known for its vibrant culinary scene. Many restaurants here offer traditional Costa Rican dishes that are family-friendly and delicious, such as casado (a typical dish that includes rice, beans, salad, and your choice of meat) or gallo pinto (a classic breakfast dish of rice and beans).

Day 2: Explore San José's Museums and Markets

San José has several attractions that are both educational and entertaining for families. Start your day with a visit to the Museo de los Niños (Children's Museum), an interactive museum located in a former military prison. The museum is designed to engage children of all ages with hands-on exhibits covering a wide range of topics, including science, technology, history, and the arts. It's a fun and educational experience that will keep the kids entertained while they learn.

After the museum, head to the Mercado Central (Central Market) for a taste of local culture. This bustling market is a sensory delight, with vibrant colors, enticing aromas, and a lively atmosphere. You can explore the market stalls, sample tropical fruits, and pick up some souvenirs. It's also a great place to try some traditional Costa Rican snacks, like empanadas or churros.

In the afternoon, visit the Museo Nacional de Costa Rica (National Museum of Costa Rica), which offers a fascinating overview of the country's history and culture. The museum is housed in a historic building that was once a military barracks, and its exhibits cover everything from pre-Columbian artifacts to Costa Rica's journey to becoming a peaceful and democratic nation. The museum's butterfly garden is a highlight, where kids can observe these beautiful insects up close.

Day 3: Travel to Tortuguero

On the third day, your family will head to the Caribbean coast to visit Tortuguero National Park, a remote and unique destination known for its rich biodiversity and important sea turtle nesting sites. The journey to Tortuguero is an adventure in itself, involving a scenic drive through the Braulio Carrillo National Park followed by a boat ride through the canals of Tortuguero. The boat ride is a wonderful opportunity to spot wildlife, including birds, monkeys, and even caimans.

Upon arrival in Tortuguero, check into your lodge and take some time to relax. The lodges in Tortuguero are often located in the jungle, providing an immersive experience in nature. Spend the rest of the day exploring the small village of Tortuguero or enjoying the lodge's amenities, such as a swimming pool or guided nature walks.

Day 4: Exploring Tortuguero National Park

Tortuguero National Park is a paradise for wildlife lovers, and it offers a variety of family-friendly activities. Start your day with a guided boat tour through the park's canals. The early morning hours are the best time to observe wildlife, as the animals are most active at this time. Your guide will help you spot creatures like howler monkeys, sloths, toucans, and possibly even manatees. The boat tour is a peaceful and fascinating way to experience the natural beauty of Tortuguero.

After the boat tour, you can explore the park further by taking a guided hike through the jungle. The trails in Tortuguero are relatively easy and provide a chance to see more of the park's diverse flora and fauna. The guides are knowledgeable about the local ecosystem and will share interesting facts and stories that will captivate both adults and children.

In the afternoon, relax at your lodge or take a stroll along the beach. If you're visiting during the sea turtle nesting season (from July to October), you can join a guided night tour to witness the incredible sight of sea turtles laying their eggs on the beach. This is a once-in-a-lifetime experience that will leave a lasting impression on the whole family.

Day 5: Whitewater Rafting on the Sarapiquí River

On day five, your family will leave Tortuguero and head to the Sarapiquí region, known for its lush rainforests and thrilling whitewater rafting opportunities. The Sarapiquí River offers rapids that are suitable for families, providing just the right amount of excitement without being too intense. The drive to Sarapiquí takes you through scenic countryside, with views of banana plantations and dense forests.

Upon arrival, you'll meet your rafting guides and receive a safety briefing before setting off on your adventure. The rafting trip on the Sarapiquí River is a fun and exhilarating experience, with rapids ranging from class II to class III. As you navigate the river's twists and turns, you'll be surrounded by beautiful scenery, including towering trees and vibrant wildlife. There will be opportunities to stop along the riverbank to swim or relax in natural pools.

After your rafting adventure, check into your accommodation in the Sarapiquí region. Many lodges here are set in the heart of the rainforest, offering a tranquil environment and the chance to spot more wildlife right from your doorstep.

Day 6: Nature and Wildlife in Sarapiquí

The Sarapiquí region is a haven for nature lovers, and day six is dedicated to exploring its rich biodiversity. Start your day with a visit to the La Selva Biological Station, a renowned research facility and nature reserve that offers guided tours for visitors. The reserve is home to a staggering variety of plants and animals, including over 400 species of birds. The guided tour takes you through primary and secondary rainforest, where you can learn about the ecology of the area and observe wildlife such as monkeys, sloths, and colorful frogs.

In the afternoon, visit the Tirimbina Rainforest Center, which offers a variety of educational and recreational activities for families. You can take a guided hike through the rainforest, cross suspension bridges over the Sarapiquí River, and participate in a chocolate tour, where you'll learn about the history and process of making chocolate from cacao beans. The chocolate tour is especially popular with kids, as it includes hands-on activities and, of course, plenty of chocolate tasting.

In the evening, consider joining a night walk to experience the rainforest after dark. The forest comes alive at night, with nocturnal creatures such as frogs, insects, and bats making their appearances. It's a unique and exciting way to explore the rainforest and discover a different side of Sarapiquí's wildlife.

Day 7: Travel to Arenal Volcano

On the seventh day, your family will travel to the Arenal Volcano region, one of Costa Rica's most iconic destinations. The drive to Arenal takes about three hours, and along the way, you'll pass through picturesque landscapes of rolling hills, farmland, and small villages.

Upon arrival in the town of La Fortuna, which is situated at the base of Arenal Volcano, you'll be greeted by the sight of the towering volcano. Although Arenal has been in a resting phase since 2010, it remains an impressive and awe-inspiring natural landmark.

After checking into your accommodation, spend the afternoon exploring the area or relaxing in one of the many hot springs that are naturally heated by the geothermal activity of the volcano. The hot springs are a favorite activity for families, offering a relaxing and fun way to unwind.

Tabacón Hot Springs is one of the most luxurious options, but there are also more budget-friendly choices like Baldi Hot Springs or Eco Termales.

Day 8: Adventure in Arenal

Arenal is a hub for outdoor activities, making it the perfect place to spend a day full of adventure. Start your day with a visit to the Arenal Volcano National Park, where you can hike along trails that wind through the rainforest and across old lava fields. The trails in the park offer stunning views of the volcano and the surrounding countryside, and they are suitable for families with children. Along the way, you may spot wildlife such as monkeys, coatis, and a variety of birds.

After your hike, head to La Fortuna Waterfall, one of the most beautiful waterfalls in Costa Rica. The waterfall is located just a short drive from La Fortuna, and a well-maintained trail leads you down to the base of the falls. The powerful cascade plunges 70 meters into a clear pool, surrounded by dense jungle. You can take a refreshing swim in the cool waters or simply relax and enjoy the natural beauty of the area.

In the afternoon, take a hanging bridges tour in the Mistico Arenal Hanging Bridges Park. This series of suspension bridges and well-maintained trails takes you through the rainforest canopy, offering a unique perspective on the flora and fauna of the region. The hanging bridges are a great way for the whole family to experience the rainforest from above, and they provide plenty of opportunities for wildlife spotting.

Day 9: Canyoning and Chocolate Tour in Arenal

On day nine, your family will experience the thrill of canyoning, also known as canyoneering, in the Arenal region. Canyoning involves navigating through a canyon by rappelling down waterfalls, jumping into pools, and climbing over rocks. It's an activity that combines adventure with the beauty of nature, making it perfect for families with older children.

The day begins with a transfer to the canyoning site, where you'll meet your guides and receive a safety briefing. After gearing up, you'll start your descent into the canyon, rappelling down a series of waterfalls ranging from 20 to 200 feet in height. The experience is exhilarating, as you lower yourself down the waterfalls, feeling the cool water cascading over you. In between rappels, there are opportunities to swim in natural pools and hike through the jungle.

After your canyoning adventure, take some time to relax and have lunch before heading to a chocolate tour in the afternoon. The Rainforest Chocolate Tour offers a fun and educational experience where you'll learn about the history and process of making chocolate from cacao beans. The tour includes hands-on activities, such as grinding cacao beans and making your own chocolate, which is a hit with kids and adults alike.

Day 10: Travel to Monteverde

On the tenth day, your family will leave the volcanic landscapes of Arenal and make your way to the mystical cloud forests of Monteverde. The drive to Monteverde takes about three to four hours and includes some bumpy roads, but the journey is well worth it. The change in scenery is dramatic as you ascend into the cool, misty heights of the cloud forest.

Monteverde is famous for its unique cloud forest ecosystem, where the high altitude and constant mist create a lush, verdant environment teeming with biodiversity. Upon arrival, visit the Monteverde Butterfly Garden or the Bat Jungle for a closer look at some of the smaller inhabitants of the cloud forest.

In the evening, consider joining a night walk tour to experience the cloud forest after dark. The forest comes alive at night, with nocturnal creatures such as frogs, insects, and possibly even a kinkajou making appearances. The night walk is a fun and educational activity for families, offering a different perspective on the cloud forest's wildlife.

Day 11: Exploring Monteverde Cloud Forest

Monteverde offers endless opportunities for adventure and exploration, and day eleven is dedicated to immersing yourself in the natural wonders of the cloud forests. Begin your day with a visit to the Monteverde Cloud Forest Reserve, one of the most renowned cloud forests in the world. The reserve is home to a staggering variety of plants, animals, and birds, including the elusive resplendent quetzal.

Take a guided hike through the reserve, where you'll learn about the delicate balance of this ecosystem and the efforts to conserve it. The trails are well-marked and range from easy to moderate, making them accessible to most visitors. The Sendero Bosque Nuboso (Cloud Forest Trail) is a popular option, offering a good mix of scenery and wildlife spotting opportunities.

After your hike, visit the Santa Elena Cloud Forest Reserve, another beautiful reserve in the area. While similar to the Monteverde Cloud Forest Reserve, Santa Elena is slightly higher in elevation and tends to be less crowded, offering a more tranquil experience. The trails here are well-maintained, and the reserve is a great place to spot birds, including hummingbirds and trogons.

Day 12: Travel to Manuel Antonio

On day twelve, it's time to leave the cool cloud forests behind and head to the warm, sun-soaked beaches of Manuel Antonio on the Pacific coast. The drive to Manuel Antonio takes about four to five hours, but the journey offers beautiful views as you descend from the mountains to the coast.

Manuel Antonio is one of Costa Rica's most popular beach destinations, and for good reason. The area is home to Manuel Antonio National Park, a small but biodiverse park that combines lush rainforest with stunning beaches. After checking into your accommodation, spend the afternoon exploring the park's trails and beaches.

The park's main trail leads to several picturesque beaches, including Playa Manuel Antonio, which is often considered one of the most beautiful beaches in Costa Rica. The clear, turquoise waters are perfect for swimming, snorkeling, or simply relaxing on the sand. As you explore the park, keep an eye out for wildlife such as sloths, monkeys, and colorful birds.

In the evening, take a stroll along Playa Espadilla, a long stretch of beach just outside the park, where you can watch the sunset over the Pacific Ocean. There are plenty of beachfront restaurants where you can enjoy fresh seafood and tropical cocktails while taking in the views.

Day 13: Beach and Adventure in Manuel Antonio

Your penultimate day in Costa Rica is all about relaxation and adventure in Manuel Antonio. Start your day with a leisurely breakfast, and then head back to Manuel Antonio National Park for more exploration. You might choose to revisit one of the beaches, take another hike, or simply enjoy the peaceful surroundings.

If you're looking for more adventure, consider taking a kayaking tour through the nearby mangroves or going on a catamaran cruise, which often includes snorkeling and the chance to see dolphins and other marine life.

For those who prefer to stay on land, horseback riding tours are available, offering a unique way to explore the surrounding countryside. You can ride through the forest, along the beach, or to a nearby waterfall, all while enjoying the natural beauty of the area.

As the day winds down, take some time to reflect on your journey through Costa Rica. Whether you choose to spend your final evening enjoying a quiet dinner or watching the sunset from a beachside bar, you'll leave with memories of a diverse and enchanting country that has something to offer every traveler.

Day 14: Departure

On the final day of your adventure-filled itinerary, you'll return to San José for your departure. Depending on your flight time, you may have some extra hours in the morning to enjoy the beach or do some last-minute shopping for souvenirs. As you leave Costa Rica, you'll carry with you the memories of an incredible journey, filled with adventure, awe-inspiring landscapes, and unforgettable experiences.

This 14-day itinerary for families in Costa Rica offers a comprehensive and enjoyable exploration of the country's diverse natural beauty and cultural experiences. From the wild canals of Tortuguero and the rich biodiversity of Sarapiquí to the majestic Arenal Volcano, the misty cloud forests of Monteverde, and the sun-kissed beaches of Manuel Antonio, this journey is designed to create lasting memories for the entire family. Costa Rica is a destination that captures the hearts of those who visit, and this itinerary ensures that every member of your family will leave with a deep appreciation for its natural wonders and warm hospitality.

CONCLUSION

As we reach the conclusion of this guide, it's clear that Costa Rica offers a truly unique and enriching experience for every kind of traveler. Whether you're seeking adventure, relaxation, or cultural exploration, this beautiful country has something special to offer. From the misty cloud forests of Monteverde to the sun-soaked beaches of Manuel Antonio, and from the vibrant markets of San José to the serene wildlife reserves of Tortuguero, Costa Rica's diverse landscapes and welcoming people make it an unforgettable destination.

This guide has aimed to provide you with all the information you need to plan a remarkable journey through Costa Rica. The itineraries and recommendations included here are designed to help you make the most of your visit, whether you're traveling with family, seeking thrills, or simply looking to unwind in a paradise that balances nature and comfort.

As you embark on your journey, remember that the true magic of Costa Rica lies in its details—the sound of howler monkeys at dawn, the sight of a resplendent quetzal in the cloud forest, the taste of fresh coffee grown on volcanic soil, and the warmth of the Ticos who are always ready to share a smile and a story. Embrace the spirit of Pura Vida, and let the beauty of Costa Rica inspire and rejuvenate you.

Thank you for choosing this guide as your companion. May your travels through Costa Rica be filled with wonder, joy, and memories that will last a lifetime. Safe travels, and hasta luego—until we meet again.

MAP OF COSTA RICA

To make your exploration of Costa Rica even easier, here is a QR code that takes you to a map. This code will help you find your way to the top attractions, accommodations, restaurants, and more with just a quick scan.

How to Use the QR Codes:
1. Open the camera app on your smartphone or tablet.
2. Point your camera at the QR code.
3. Tap the notification that appears on your screen to open the location in Google Maps.
4. Search for your desired destination.

SCAN THE QR CODE BELOW

Made in United States
Orlando, FL
06 January 2025